Three Picassos
before Breakfast

THREE PICASSOS BEFORE BREAKFAST

MEMOIRS OF AN ART FORGER'S WIFE

BY

Anne-Marie Stein

AS TOLD TO

George Carpozi, Jr.

HAWTHORN BOOKS, INC.

PUBLISHERS / *New York*

"David Stein's work in perfecting the style of the masters may properly be ascribed to that special talent with which true artists are uniquely endowed. . . ."

Justice Arnold L. Fein
New York State Supreme Court

CONTENTS

Three Picassos
before Breakfast

1

MEETING
MY MAN

As I sit now and recount my memories of my brief happy-tragic life with David Stein, I cannot decide whether he brought more joy or sadness into my world. Nor am I certain whether to thank or take to task my old friend Harry Metz, who introduced me to David during my Easter vacation in Cannes in 1964. At the time I was studying law at the university in Aix-en-Provence. Though spring had arrived and the severity of the mistral winds that buffet us during the long winters had subsided, I felt a chill in my bones and the urge to return to the warmth and world of excitement on the Côte d'Azur.

The weather was not my only excuse to get away. In my own foolish, impetuous way I had fallen in love with a terribly urbane, witty, and irresistible lawyer who had a prominent practice—as well as a wife—in my hometown. I had known from the beginning that it was an impossible situation, yet the fascination of cavorting clandestinely with such a man, fifteen years older than I but so incomparably cultured and romantic, prompted me to succumb to my own better judgment and to ignore the lessons imposed on me by a strict mother and a disciplinarian-minded father who had served with distinction in the diplomatic corps.

All my previous excursions to Cannes had been in the company of my ex-lover, but now the group on the outing comprised Marlou and some of our friends from Avignon. Even as I watched the beauties and buffoons playing out their roles in the midst of the beautiful people who had come to the Côte d'Azur to pay tribute to the movie of the year, *Les Parapluies de Cherbourg*, I felt desperately unhappy. The memory of so much gaiety and laughter on my earlier sojourns on the Riviera made me melancholy and morose.

Only when I ran into Harry Metz, a Dutch real-estate broker to whom I had been introduced on one of my previous visits to Cannes, did my state of mind take a turn for the better. By now Harry had given up his lucrative business and had become an art dealer as well as a patron of the arts, a step that in time led him to near bankruptcy. Harry invited my sister and me to have an aperitif with him at a café on the Croisette along the beach. As we were sipping our drinks, Harry recognized someone strolling past our table. He was a heavy-set man with a full, round, and very handsome face who greatly resembled Orson Welles. Harry called him over and introduced us.

"I want you to meet a friend," Harry said. "This is David Stein. . . ."

When David sat at our table, I sensed an immediate and overpowering attraction to him. There was something about his manner that got under my skin, and when he glanced into my eyes, I was enchanted by his warmth and charm. There was something hurried about him, too.

"Why don't you all come up to my apartment and listen to music?" he suggested.

We had been in his suite in the Canberra hardly an hour listening to Mozart, Beethoven, and Bach when David all at once turned to me and asked if I would go to dinner with him. More than anything, I wanted to accept the invitation, but I had a date that night that I couldn't break. I suggested that David take Marlou instead, and they went out that night.

The next day he took my sister on a little business trip to Monte Carlo, but that evening, I was the one whom David asked to dinner. We went to a very intimate, cozy, candlelit restaurant in *la vieille ville*. The dinner was perfect. I remember the menu as though we were still seated at the table—avocado, broiled baby lamb chops, salad, and, oh, so much Beaujolais. The romantic atmosphere was enhanced tenfold by strolling musicians who frequently stopped to play at our table.

After we left the restaurant, David took me to a discotheque, but the loud, strident sounds of rock 'n' roll did nothing for us. I was not crazy about dancing, nor was David. So we spent the time talking about life—and about art. Especially about art, for Harry Metz had told me that David was in some way involved in selling paintings to art dealers. I had no idea then, nor for a good time to come, precisely what his merchantry in paintings consisted of.

After we left the discotheque and David took me to his apartment in the Canberra, I began to think of him in terms of a permanent relationship. Although I knew very little about him, I saw the same qualities in David that had attracted me to my former lover, the lawyer from Avignon. David was absolutely fascinating in every sense of the word, and what made him all the more attractive to me was that he was not married. David had the stamp of exclusivity that had been totally lacking in my previous relationship.

I remained with David until two in the morning, and when he finally took me back to my room in the Carlton, my head was aswim with the names of Picasso, Braque, Klee, Kandinsky, Chagall, and Miró, and many other modern masters. All through the night I had been spellbound by my teacher's rhapsodic testimonials to the men who had created the works of beauty dominating this century's artistic culture. I could not resist his invitation to accompany him the next day on his rounds of the galleries in Cannes and to see firsthand many of the works of these noted painters.

After transitory visits to several galleries, David took me to the Galerie Art de France. David sought out the owner of the gallery, Monsieur Aubry, and proffered to sell him a collection of paintings in the possession of an architect who had retained David in his capacity as a *courtier en peintures* (broker in paintings) to dispose of his works. While I observed David and Monsieur Aubry in their discussions from a discreet distance, I could not help but feel that the two men were old friends, for they chatted with such fervor and amiability. Yet I was astonished to learn after leaving the gallery that that was not the case at all.

"It was the first time I ever met or talked with the old fossil," David confided in me.

This was an early insight that I acquired into David's personality. His overwhelming warmth, charm, and glibness made people he met for the first time fall prey to his allurement. His craftiness was camouflaged by cajolery and confabulation, a tactical ploy that worked on his victims every time. Yet David's manner was as natural as the tender and gracious plants in the Garden of Versailles. He was a born charmer, and his courtesy, civility, politeness, and etiquette were habits that he had acquired and nurtured through all of the twenty-nine years of his life.

Despite all of David's exercise of wile and salesmanship, he was unable to interest Monsieur Aubry in the architect's collection of paintings. When he realized that he was not going to make a sale, David used another tactic: He offered to sell some of the paintings in the Galerie Art de France. Monsieur Aubry consented and even went so far as to give David one painting by Bernard Buffet on consignment. I remember it very well—it was a huge oil, an absolute monstrosity, depicting a nude woman with a hydropic swollen stomach and the face of Bernard Buffet. David knew he could never sell the painting but consented to take it with him to beguile Monsieur Aubry and keep the door open at the gallery for future transactions.

When we left, David told me that he had one other stop to make, at the art gallery in the Majestic Hotel.

"But before we go there," David said, "I want to stop at my hotel."

I went up to his apartment with him and watched as he unwrapped the Buffet and hung it over the couch.

"There," he smiled, "doesn't that make the room look homier?"

Bad as I thought the painting was, I could not deny that it had improved the room. Although it was ugly, it gave the room a personal touch. After all, it was a ten-thousand-dollar work of art.

The visit to the Majestic Gallery was more productive. The owner, Monsieur Domenico, expressed interest in one of the architect's paintings, a small Van Dongen portrait of a woman from the flapper era sitting in a chair and covered with ostrich feathers. But one hitch held up the sale.

"I will require authentication of the painting," Monsieur Domenico said.

He then explained how easily that could be obtained. All that David had to do was go to Monte Carlo, show the painting to Van Dongen at his home there, and have him verify in writing that this was one of his works.

When we returned to the Canberra, David phoned Van Dongen's house and spoke to his wife, who asked him to bring the painting over on Sunday (this was Thursday). Then David turned to me.

"Well, that's all the business I have to do this week. Now let us go out and have some fun."

After stopping at my hotel and changing into a black evening dress, I went with David to the opening of the Whisky à Go-Go, the biggest nightclub on the Riviera. We were accompanied to the gala by Harry Metz and his date, and we feasted and frolicked into the early morning hours. After our foursome formation broke up, David took me to his apartment and made love to me, and I spent the night with him. By now I was fully convinced that David was a special kind of man. I was very much in love with him.

On Easter Sunday morning David and I drove to Van Dongen's house in Harry's car. Madame Van Dongen admitted us to the living room and quickly let us know in her smartly clipped British accent that she was all business. By now Van Dongen was pushing eighty, and she was apparently handling most of the negotiations involving the sale of his paintings, as well as authentication.

"The fee is two hundred dollars," she told David. I didn't realize it then, but I know now what she meant.

Since this was a small watercolor that could have commanded no more than five hundred dollars, David didn't think it was worth the two-hundred-dollar outlay. He apologized to Madame Van Dongen for the inconvenience, and we left.

On the drive back I asked David what he planned to do.

"I think I'll make up that little piece of paper with Van Dongen's signature myself."

I was shocked. "You're absolutely crazy," I protested. "That's a felony. You'll go to jail."

David smiled. "I'm only joking," he assured me. To this day I don't know whether he forged the authentication, but he did sell the painting to Domenico. When I asked him how he had managed to sell it, David replied, "Well, I explained to Domenico that it would have cost too much for the authentication, and he accepted that."

As I learned later, even an artist himself who cannot identify a painting of his own from a fake might, for a fee, authenticate an imitation of his own work.

The day after Easter, I put my sister on the train for Avignon. She was not shocked that I was not returning home, for she could see that I had fallen in love with David and that I intended to live with him.

"What am I going to tell Mama and Papa?" she asked in a quandary.

"Just tell them that I am enjoying myself so much that I have decided to stay a while longer," I suggested.

After seeing Marlou off, I returned to the Canberra. I could not go back to the Carlton, for I had moved into David's suite by now. David was waiting for me.

"*Chérie*," he said with a smile, "we are going to take a drive out to the country."

We took a lazy ride along picturesque winding roads to the town of St.-Paul-de-Vence where an artist who was going to figure very prominently in our lives a few years later had his home. The man was the aging master Marc Chagall, but we had not gone there to see him. David was bound for a small gallery owned by André Verdet, the poet who had written a book about another master, the late Jean Cocteau. Because of his authorship of that book, Verdet came to be regarded as an authority on Cocteau's works. And now David wanted Verdet to authenticate a dozen Cocteau drawings that he wanted to sell.

Verdet examined the sketches, commented on how very good they were, and signed his name to the backs of them.

"I would not do this," he said, "if they were not genuine."

As I was to learn at a much later time, all twelve of those Cocteaus were fakes. David had sketched them.

David had one other stop to make before we returned to Cannes—the Galerie de Ville Franche Sur Mer, next door to the small chapel that had been decorated by Cocteau. When the artist was alive, the gallery obtained his works directly from Cocteau. Now that the master was dead, the gallery was anxious to obtain Cocteaus from any source. David knew that, and that was why he brought the drawings there.

When the owner of the gallery saw Verdet's authentication on the pieces, he bought all twelve without uttering the slightest protest about the price. David had asked for $2,500, and that was what he received.

With this sale, the money he had received from Monsieur Domenico for the Van Dongen, and a few other transactions he had made before I had met him, David's pockets were bulging with cash.

"I have a wonderful thought," David whispered in my ear that night in our suite at the Canberra. "Why don't we go to Paris? You know, I still have these paintings that I haven't sold for my client [the architect]. There is a much better opportunity to dispose of them there and to get a better price."

Knowing David as well as I do now, his desire to leave Cannes was precipitated only by an awareness that he had no outlets left on the Riviera to peddle his own fakes—not the architect's legitimate works.

The thought of going to Paris thrilled me. I had been there before but never with someone as charming, fascinating, and romantic as David. We took one of the fast luxury trains that link the Riviera with the French capital, and the next morning we registered as husband and wife at the Hôtel Lutetia, an old hostelry but one of the finest on the Left Bank.

Our first few days were glorious ones as David took me on one whirlwind tour of the city after another. I was feeling even closer to David now because we had spent so many long, leisurely hours together. We seemed to share the same inordinate interest in literature, music, and painting. David and I always seemed to be on the same wavelength, intellectually and emotionally.

During our first week in Paris David seemed to pay only the slightest interest to business. Minimal as it may have been, though, the time he devoted to his work was always well spent. For on every sight-seeing or shopping excursion, David made it a point to stop at one or another of the scores of art galleries that dot the city and to build up a dossier in his mind of exactly what types of works they were buying and what price range they were dealing in.

"Good day, monsieur," David would greet the art dealers in the various galleries, "can you tell me what particular pieces you might be interested in?"

Invariably there was someone who wanted something: a Chagall or two, perhaps a few Cocteau drawings, a Braque or a Miró; others were in the market for the works of Derain or Calder, and some expressed a desire to obtain something special from Bonnard, Marie Laurencin, or, most certainly, Picasso.

Although these visits took only minutes and did little to interrupt the casual itinerary of our holiday, they served to prepare David for the "big kill." He was operating like a general on the battlefront. First he would scout the "enemy," then he would turn to his "maps" and plot the attack. Finally, he would storm the bastions with swift and slashing totality. It would all be over in minutes. And the art dealer or gallery would feel absolutely no pain. They had parted with their money and gained a work of art that they truly believed was legitimate. Or did they?

In looking back now on David's peripatetic career as an art forger, I cannot in all honesty say that some of the galleries and dealers who did business with my "husband" were not unaware that he was selling forgeries.

The truth of the matter is that there are dealers and galleries that trade in works of art with absolutely no conscience—nor with any aesthetic appreciation of the paintings. They are bound up only in the materialistic thirst to make money. More money. And still more money. That is why many of those who bought David's forgeries knew full well what they were buying. But David's work was very good. Sometimes he painted his fakes too well— better than the masters could. And these had to be disposed of, a job that became my exclusive province. We could have made hundreds of thousands of dollars more just from the paintings I shredded with shears into tiny little pieces and flushed down the toilets of hotels, motels, furnished rooms, and apartments.

But David was a perfectionist. The piece he forged had to be precisely right, nothing less and nothing more. Once he had composed his work (he never made a direct copy of any master's painting but merely stole elements from each and fabricated his own creation that had a striking resemblance to the artist's style), David was convinced that the piece was exactly what the painter himself would have produced.

That in essence is why neither David nor I ever suffered any pangs of conscience for having duped the gallery owners, art dealers, and collectors who bought our works. Those few who knew the difference did not seem to mind at all, in fact, they were glad to get them.

What David Stein perpetrated upon the art world was a brilliantly engineered, masterfully executed hoax. It was illegal, but he did not deserve to be treated like a criminal, and he certainly should not have been jailed for four years. But that is what happened, and that is why I am writing this book.

2

MY FIRST SALE AND
MY FIRST PREGNANCY

Psychology always figured prominently in any of David's transactions with art galleries, dealers, or individual collectors. With
his uncanny ability to evaluate human behavior and predict its
course, it was only natural that David should elect to employ me
as a *courtière en peintures*. In plain English, I became a front for
him.

My first excursion into the realm of vending art occurred during our second week in Paris when David decided to unload some
of the architect's consignment on the respected Galerie Maeght.
Though the paintings were legitimate and desirable pieces,
David had concluded that I would have a much better chance of
selling to Maeght than he.

First of all, he reasoned, I am a pretty woman. In France, as
in any other country, that is an important asset, and it always
puts you ahead in the game of connivance. But this particular
venture bore no shades of underhandedness. David simply didn't
think he could do as well as a sweet, innocent-looking, green-
eyed French girl in interesting Maeght in this specific group of
paintings. He thought that the gallery would be reluctant to buy
from him because they were aware of his sales to some of Paris's
more celebrated galleries. If David walked into Maeght with the

architect's works—most of them unimpressive, small watercolors and pen-and-ink drawings—they were likely to think, "Oh, he's probably been around to the other galleries, and they refused them." But if he sent me in, posing as a representative of a private collector, then Maeght was likely to go for them.

Rehearsed by David for long hours, I finally went to the gallery with the architect's collection. Of course, I refused to talk with anyone but the owner himself.

"Oh, Monsieur Maeght," I said when he came out, "I just came into possession of these paintings, and I don't know anything about them. But I know what the name Maeght means to the world of art, and that is why I have come to you. . . ."

This was an intentional juxtaposition of credit for the gallery owner, for it was not he but his father who commanded the greater respect and admiration of the art world. Aimé Maeght happened to be the renowned dealer representing Chagall, Kandinsky, Braque, Miró, Derain, Calder, and Bonnard.

But young Monsieur Maeght almost popped the buttons of his vest as he bloated with elation over my encomium to the name of Maeght. He took an immediate interest in the works I was trying to peddle.

"Please tell me, Monsieur Maeght, how much are they worth?" I pleaded with a put-on wide-eyed naïveté.

"About fourteen hundred for the whole lot," he answered.

I couldn't help but feel an intensified admiration and love for David. Before I left our room at the Lutetia, he had said to me, "*Chérie*, take nothing less than a thousand dollars, but if you are as persuasive as I think you are, you should skin him for fourteen hundred."

David had also alerted me to adopt the pose of a reluctant salesman. This was important. For if I had shown anxiety to sell the paintings, Maeght would probably have come up with a much lower estimate of their worth. As it was, I had told Maeght that I wasn't looking to sell the paintings but just to determine what their value was. But I could see he wanted to buy them.

"Yes," he replied when I asked the question, "I would be interested in them."

"Well," I said, "let me think awhile about it. I'm not certain that I want to part with them."

I went back to the hotel, and David told me he was proud of the way I had handled myself. A week later, on a signal from David, I phoned Maeght and told him I had decided to sell the paintings.

"Bring them in," he said.

Maeght took a second, hard look at the lot and decided to buy a half-dozen. He wrote a check for eight hundred dollars, and I returned to David with the remaining six paintings, which he sold the next day for seven hundred dollars to the Galerie des Saints Pères.

That night, David and I left the Hôtel Lutetia and moved to a small hotel on the Boulevard St. Michel, where we registered under fictitious names. David was terrified when he heard that I had spoken to my sister on the phone and told here where I was. He was fearful that my father would come after me and drag me home.

In our smaller, cramped room I became more aware of David's large portfolio, which I had always assumed was crammed with paintings and drawings that he was seeking to sell for his clients. But when I finally looked into it one day after I found it staring me in the face, it was empty. I was puzzled.

I was even more puzzled over the next several days when David would return to our room with an ear-to-ear grin and almost shout, "*Alors!* I sold four more Chagalls today." Or, "*Chérie*, they bought two Van Dongens and a Marie Laurencin without any bargaining."

Though the thought was always in the back of my mind to ask David where he was getting the paintings he was selling, I never got around to it because from the moment he came back to me there was always so much else to talk about—and do.

We had been in Paris exactly a month when David awakened me in the middle of the night.

"*Chérie*," he said softly as he cuddled up to me in our bed, "what would you say if I told you we are going to Biarritz for a vacation?"

"But I thought this was our vacation," I said naïvely.

"You won't know what a vacation is like until you have been in Biarritz," he said as he wrapped his arms around me.

Biarritz was beautiful. Though it was winter, the climate was admirably warm. What wonderful memories I have of the place— David and I walking barefoot along the promenade from the sandy Grand Plage, the Côte des Basques, and the Promontoire du Halde. The most beautiful sight was the Côte des Basques and its endless foaming breakers that have given rise to the name Côte d'Argent, which is applied to the whole of the French Basque coast.

Our stay in Biarritz was glorious, but what I remember most about that part of our adventure was our stopover in St.-Jean-de-Luz, just south of the famed watering spa in the southwest of France. David rented a car, and we drove over rugged, steep roads that rose in short, tight curves up the foothills of the Pyrenees Mountains toward the border with Spain. We were headed for St.-Jean-Pied-de-Port.

Tears came to my eyes as I listened to why David had wanted to visit that town. During World War II his half-brother, François, a mere sixteen, decided to join the French Free Forces being organized by General Charles de Gaulle in England. He apparently made his way safely through occupied France to St.-Jean-Pied-de-Port but was captured by the Nazis before he could cross into Spain. François was never heard from again. His mother spent many years after the war trying to find him. The search was in vain. What scant clues she unearthed pointed to an uncertain fate, but she had to settle for that because there was nothing else.

"My mother believes François was sent to the concentration camp in Oranienburg and that he died there," David told me, his eyes staring blankly at the rugged mountain ranges that form the border with Spain. "What a tragedy if he was captured here," David went on in a choked voice. "He was so near to freedom."

Though there was a ten-year age difference between them, David had felt a special closeness and deep affection toward François. David was only going on seven when François left to join the Free Forces, but his warm remembrances of his half-brother are indelible. That was why he had to make the pilgrimage to St.-Jean-Pied-de-Port and pay tribute to François's memory.

I don't know whether David prayed, because I have never known the attitude of the body to reflect the soul when it is on its knees.

We remained in St.-Jean-de-Luz nearly two weeks. During that period I read many of the books that we had picked up in Paris in a conscientious effort to broaden my knowledge about modern painters and their works. If I were to share duties with David as a *courtière en peintures*, I thought that I should become better acquainted with the masters and their painting styles, and David was delighted that I had taken such an interest in his work and shown a voluntariness to prepare myself for other exercises in selling, following my coup with the Galerie Maeght.

My reading and the lessons I learned from David soon enabled me to recognize the styles of most modern painters, to identify many of their works at a glance, and in many instances even to distinguish the different periods of such artists as Picasso, Braque, and Vlaminck. That last accomplishment was the most challenging, for it involved an ability to detect clues in the masterpieces that mirror the era in which the artists produced their works.

"*Magnifique!*" David would shout triumphantly whenever I correctly identified some obscure point in one painting or another, or glibly associated the work with the particular stage of the artist's life when it was painted. David's enthusiasm over how much I was learning in my cram-course could hardly be contained. Nor could mine. David was very proud of me, and I was proud of myself.

Finally our holiday in St.-Jean-de-Luz ended, and we went to Bordeaux for business. On the way down from Paris, David and I had stopped at this port city of southwest France to scout the Galerie la Crémaillère. David was told they were mainly in the market for Cocteaus, and he promised them he would try to obtain some of Cocteau's drawings on his rounds.

Between the time we left the Galerie la Crémaillère and the moment we returned there, David had not gone to a single gallery nor made contact with any collector. He was with me almost every minute of the day and night. That togetherness might also serve to explain why I was feeling so sick when we went back to Bordeaux and checked into the Grand Hôtel Montre. I didn't yet know what was wrong with me, but I just couldn't eat.

I had had that same feeling a few days before at breakfast in the restaurant at St.-Jean-de-Luz. I reflected now with somewhat more sobriety at the remark the waitress had cast in jest when she heard me say I wasn't feeling well.

"Maybe you're pregnant," she kidded. I laughed then, and so did David. Now in Bordeaux I was beginning to wonder.

I also did some wondering about the five Cocteau drawings that David brought into the Galerie la Crémaillère and sold for fifty dollars apiece. I had not seen them in his portfolio, and I knew he could not have obtained them from any source. Yet my curiosity—it was not suspicion at this point—was aroused only momentarily, and I felt no compulsion to press David for an explanation.

Whatever thoughts I had about the five Cocteaus were quickly driven away by the conversation between David and the gallery owner after the transaction for the five drawings came to a close. As a point of information, David had asked the gallery owner if he knew of anyone who might be interested in a Van Dongen.

"It is so strange that you should ask," the man smiled. "Only this morning I received a call from my good friend who owns a gallery in Toulouse, and he is desperate for Van Dongens."

Since Toulouse was only about 160 miles northwest and less than a three-hour train ride away, David decided that he would pay a visit to the Galerie Chappe-Lautier. But before leaving the gallery in Bordeaux, David had impressed the owner to such an extent that he was entrusted with two of La Crémaillère's most important painting consignments. These included a very pretty and delicate Marie Laurencin watercolor and an exquisite portfolio of Dunoyer de Segonzacs.

"Since you are going to Paris," the gallery owner told David, "I'm certain you will be able to sell them and to receive a handsome price."

David had told the owner that we were going back to Paris, but he also made it clear that we did not intend to leave Bordeaux for at least another week.

"It does not matter," the man said. "I am in no hurry to sell these paintings. Take them with you and dispose of them in your good time."

David wanted me to go with him to Toulouse, but when I awakened the next morning, my biliousness was worse than it had ever been. The mere thought of riding a train turned my stomach. David had to go alone, but he was back by nightfall. And he was twelve hundred dollars richer. Much later, I learned that those five Cocteaus and the Van Dongen were forged by David late at night while I slept in our hotel room in St.-Jean-de-Luz!

Our stay at the Grand Hôtel Montre was briefer than we had expected because of the extreme generosity of the hotel owner, who took a liking to David and me and invited us to stay at his beach house on the outskirts of Bordeaux. This came about only a day or so after we had met him for the first time in the hotel bar. He had heard David asking a waiter where he could rent a car in order to tour the vineyards of Bordeaux. No one could visit this city and ignore the beautiful fields of cultivated grapevines that have been producing the world's best wines for nearly eight centuries.

"Allow me to help out," the owner interrupted as he took a seat at our table and introduced himself as Guy de Noiret. "If you want to tour the vineyards," he offered, "I will let you use my car." Then he took the keys out of his pocket and handed them to David.

We visited the cellars where the wines are aged and bottled and were even allowed to taste many samples. All were very good. David even bought a few bottles. And when we started back to the city at the end of the day, David was a little tipsy.

The next day, the hotel owner took us to stay at his place on the Atlantic Ocean until the end of the week. Then it was time to move on. We were going back to Paris.

The song is entitled "April in Paris," but I believe someone should compose lyrics and music to pay tribute to the month of May, for Paris is even more beautiful in the late spring. Everything was alive and jumping when we arrived—except me. Although we took a room in the Hôtel Racine on the Left Bank, which was right next to the Place de l'Odéon and the Luxembourg Gardens, I found little opportunity to enjoy any of the grace and magnificence of these sights.

I was sleeping sixteen hours a day, and I still didn't know what was wrong with me. But my continuing nausea began to make me suspect that my liver was acting up, since I had always had a mild problem with it. And since David and I had been drinking liquor and wine daily, I attributed my problems to alcohol. I had no appetite for breakfast, and I couldn't smoke or even tolerate the smell of David's cigarettes. All that my stomach could bear were a cup of weak tea in the morning, a hard-boiled egg for lunch, and some bouillon in the evening.

I was suffering through my fourth day of sickness when David, who had been out all day, returned to our room. His arms were full of packages. He laid them down on the table, came over to the bed and kissed me, and then began to open the parcels. I saw him take out drawing paper, followed by pastels and tubes of gouache and watercolors. He placed everything carefully on the table and walked back to the bed. Now he was holding a small photo of the very Van Dongen that we had taken to the artist's wife for authentication. He held it up so I could see it and asked:

"What do you think it would look better in—pastel or water-color?"

I was thunderstruck. I felt numb all over, and I was speechless. David had parted the only curtain of secrecy between us. He was going to forge a painting—right before my very eyes!

3

HOW WE *FORGED*
AHEAD TOGETHER

Overcome as I was by David's stunning confession that he was a forger, I nevertheless couldn't stop myself from harboring an attitude of deep respect tinged with awe as I watched him in wide-eyed fascination bringing a Van Dongen into being. It was the most remarkable exercise in fraud that I had ever witnessed, and what made it all the more exciting was that the work David was producing bore virtually no detectable difference in style or technique from the model serving for his fake.

When David finished his work in something less than two hours, I couldn't help but feel he had created a *masterpiece*, because it looked more like the works of Van Dongen than the small original from which he had appropriated the many elements that went into his fake.

David never copied. Rather than making exact replicas of any work—which was a thousandfold more dangerous practice—David simply improvised on a theme. In this case the portrait of the woman from the flapper era who is sitting in a chair covered with ostrich feathers was given a new position in the chair by David. He also changed the other elements in Van Dongen's original version, and he changed the medium: Van Dongen's work had been done in watercolor; David did his fake with pastels.

Before I go on, let me explain why it is so very dangerous to make direct copies of any work of art. Let's set up an example with the very Von Dongen that David had sold to Monsieur Domenico at the Majestic Gallery in Cannes. Suppose Monsieur Domenico had shipped that work to the Galerie Maeght in Paris, and when we arrived in Paris David made an exact replica of that Van Dongen and took it to Maeght.

Can you imagine how quickly Monsieur Maeght would have called the French *sûreté*, once he determined that Van Dongens were being paraded to the galleries as twins? The inviolate rule that guides all artists is to never create two of a kind, even in a different medium. They may—and often do—come close to duplication when they paint a series on one theme, but there is always some significant variation from one canvas to another.

Though I stood in admiring solemnity before David that night after he had finished his beautiful forgery, I could not constrain my apprehensions and fears. I had been thinking of the possible consequences David could suffer—not only if he were unmasked as a forger but if he were to be caught trying to sell a fake. In France the mere possession of fraudulent art with intent to sell is a serious crime, even if you happen to be the victim of duplicity and do not know the piece you are trying to sell is a forgery. You will get equal punishment in both cases.

"David, you can't take such a chance," I pleaded. "If you should get caught, I would go out of my mind. I love you so much that I don't want to lose you. . . ."

David walked over to me, took me in his arms, and with a big grin said softly, "*Chérie*, my concern is very much for you. I don't think you are going to change me. I am what I am, and I intend to go on being myself. That is why I wanted you to see what I have been doing. Does it shock you?"

"Of course!" I cried out. "I never had the slightest idea that you were a forger. You don't know how paralyzed I became when you opened those pastels and began to do the Van Dongen."

Now that David had bared the last secret that had stood between us, he moved ahead to the next thought that was burning in his mind.

"Now that you know what I am doing, don't you think it would be better for you if you went back to your family?" He stared into my eyes. He wasn't smiling anymore, and I could see the anxiety etched on his face as he waited for my answer.

I took a deep breath. "David, I don't want to go anywhere," I said quickly. "I want to stay with you even though I know what you are."

David tightened his embrace and kissed me. Now at last there were no secrets between us. We had reached a complete and binding understanding. We were not only partners in the conjugal bed but confederates in a conspiracy that would in time grow into one of the most celebrated and ingenious schemes ever perpetrated on the art world.

The next day, David took his forged creation to the Galerie Epona and sold it with uncommon ease. He was paid a princely six hundred dollars—even more than Van Dongen's own piece had commanded in Cannes!

When David returned to the hotel, he found me in distress. My condition had worsened, and I was beginning to feel feverish. David prepared some bouillon, brought it to me in bed, and after I assured him that I didn't need a doctor, went to the table with the drawing paper and paints.

"This Marie Laurencin will make an excellent model," David suggested with a significant wink. He was holding the delicate painting that had been entrusted to him by the gallery in Bordeaux to sell in Paris. Of course David had every intention of selling it, as well as the Dunoyer de Segonzacs that belonged to the Galerie la Crémaillère, and to forward the proceeds to Bordeaux after deducting his 30 percent commission. But he wasn't quite ready to let the dainty watercolor leave his hands. That painting was going to give birth to a half-dozen more Marie Laurencins before it was disposed of at a gallery.

David spent the next three days turning out his prearranged quota of Marie Laurencins, and each was a gem. Even the master herself would have been impressed with David's faithful attention to detail and his painstaking care with the coloring. Perfectionist that he was and with relatively little experience, David destroyed more than two dozen partly finished and completed paintings in the style of Marie Laurencin because they did not meet his stringent specifications for excellence.

Marie Laurencin would not be happy with this one," David

would say as he tossed a reject over to me on the bed. I would then proceed to shred the painting, which had become my first assignment now that I was an accomplice in David's clandestine handiwork.

By the time David had finished the sixth of his Marie Laurencins I was in agony. I had terrible cramps, and my temperature had risen to 103°. David refused to rely on my judgment any longer. He went downstairs to the lady who owned the hotel, and she summoned her physician.

"You are having a miscarriage, my dear," I remember the doctor saying with slow emphasis. "We will have to get you to the hospital."

I need not tell you how utterly dumbfounded I was, not to mention David, to learn that I was about to lose a baby neither of us knew I was carrying.

My condition precipitated an immediate financial crisis. Since I was being taken to a private hospital, demand for payment would be made in advance, and David did not have the money.

"It is all right," Madame Desmarets, the hotel owner, comforted us, "I will advance you the money to pay the hospital." She promptly handed David a blank signed check.

At the hospital I was wheeled into surgery and given sodium pentathol, and the doctor performed a curettage. When I was wheeled out of the operating room, I half-opened my eyes and recognized David and Madame Desmarets looking down at me.

"How do you feel, ma chérie?" I heard David say.

I mumbled that I was all right.

"Do you know who I am?" David came back.

I whispered his name and through my bleary eyes saw him smile.

"Did you suffer much?" he persisted. Then there was another question and still another.

I couldn't understand why David was cross-examining me that way in my condition. But my condition was precisely the reason David was pumping me with questions. He was aware that I had been given sodium pentathol, which is truth serum. And he was trying to ascertain whether the influence of the drug had worn off—lest I babble and give away his deep, dark secret!

My stay in the hospital was a mere overnight adventure. I was discharged the next morning after what had been one of the best night's sleep I'd had in years. Back in the hotel, David tucked me into bed and brought me a bowl of soup that Madame Desmarets had sent upstairs. By early afternoon when I was resting comfortably and didn't need any more attention, David left me and went off to peddle the Marie Laurencins he had painted in order to raise the money to pay back the kindly Madame Desmarets. When he returned, he had brought back not only enough to satisfy the hospital bill but also to finance the start of a tour that would take us to many cities in many countries.

My pregnancy seemed to work a change in David. It was a change for the better which I appreciated greatly. He behaved more like a husband than a consort, and he treated me more like a wife than a mistress. My life with him was set.

From Paris we went to Lyon for a brief stay. We went sightseeing, visited a few galleries, found nothing of interest to hold us there, and went on to Montélimar, which is halfway between Lyon and Marseilles. Montélimar, which is known as the capital of the *nougat*, a delicacy made of honey, almonds, pistachios, and sugar that has a striking similarity to halvah, is a lively, thriving community. But more importantly, Montélimar was simply a convenient place to stop and paint.

We checked into the Relais de l'Empereur, and I kidded David about putting up at the "stopover of the Emperor," which referred to Napoleon, who had made this hotel his overnight encampment in the course of his journeys through the Alps between Italy and France.

"I do not plan to employ any of Bonaparte's battle tactics in this modest conquest," David kidded as he broke out his drawing paper and paints. "But I do wish, Anne-Marie, that you would tell me what you think of using mixed-media for my next Van Dongen."

Though I was still very far from being considered an art expert, I had learned a great deal about the modern masters and their works in the few months with David. And now as he was doing his fakes, David was relying on my judgment more and more.

"Pastels and watercolors will be just excellent," I agreed.

The model for David's Van Dongen once again was the photo of the painting he had sold in Cannes. Though by this time he had a number of photos of other works by this painter, David felt more secure in appropriating the theme for his forgeries from that first one, because it was one of Van Dongen's more obscure works. Thus by stealing from this lesser-known painting, he was able to create a piece that looked like a Van Dongen, yet the risk of discovery that it was a forgery was greatly reduced.

As I watched David work the watercolors and pastels onto the drawing paper bringing another Van Dongen to life, I began to feel a vicarious thrill at the thought that someone in this world would one day soon have this painting in its frame hanging in a place of honor in the living room—never knowing it was counterfeit.

Everyone, I imagine, has a bit of larceny in him, and whatever latent thievishness was bottled up in me had surfaced. I was adapting very nicely to the life of a forger's mistress. I told myself, "Anne-Marie, if this is going to be your life, then you must contribute all you can to make certain David becomes the best forger there is." For as long as I can remember, I have never been able to tolerate mediocrity. I have always adhered to the principle that if you are going to do *anything*, do it in the *best way*.

David completed the Van Dongen in our room in the Relais de l'Empereur in a couple of hours that night. In the morning he left me at the hotel because I was still convalescing and feeling somewhat weak, and went by himself to nearby Aix-en-Provence to sell the painting. When he returned later in the day, I could see by the look of elation on his face that he had made a big killing.

And what a killing it was! The Galerie Vial bought the forgery and paid David an unbelievable one thousand dollars!

"I think they liked it," said David in the understatement of 1964.

We left Montélimar by train the following day and went to Collioure, on the Mediterranean some twenty miles from the Spanish border.

4

WE MEET DALI—IN
AN OBNOXIOUS MOOD

When we arrived in Collioure, the tourists were beginning to descend on this small fishing village, which doubles as a popular vacation spa in summer. Collioure is also renowned as an artists' colony, and during World War II it served, along with Céret, another little village in the foothills of the Pyrenees, as a refuge for painters, such as Picasso, Van Dongen, Braque, Dufy, Derain, and others who had fled Paris after the occupation.

But David had not come to Collioure to paint in the style of the modern masters nor in any other style. He had brought me there for rest and recuperation and to take it easy himself. At first we had planned to stay only a few days or a week, but David got himself involved quite unintentionally in another art—moviemaking. That kept us in Collioure throughout the summer.

It all started after we met Claude Zekri, one of the owners of the town's only nightclub, next door to the house in which we were staying. Zekri, a Sephardic Jew who had to leave Algeria after De Gaulle gave the country back to the natives, was a bachelor and lived in an apartment by himself. His prime complaint was that he had to do his own cooking.

"Well, you know that we are going to be here awhile," David suggested, "and Anne-Marie is a very good cook. Why not let her prepare the meals?"

In effect, David was buying us a meal ticket. What he was thinking was: "If Anne-Marie does the cooking, we can eat at Zekri's."

Claude must have been desperate because he flipped over the idea.

Before long, we were introduced to other members of his family, including his sister, Maggy, and her husband, Henri. We found them all to be very charming.

One of Claude's secret ambitions was to produce a movie. Perhaps it was the influence of the family's association with the late actress Bella Darvi, who grew up with the Zekris in the *Rue des Rosiers*. "Street of the Rosebushes" is a very pretty name, but it also happened to be a Jewish ghetto.

But I think Claude was encouraged to make a film by the recent dramatic advances of *cinéma vérité*, which had shattered the citadels of the big moviemakers.

"Look what Jean-Luc Godard has done," Claude told us one night at a dinner of bouillabaisse, which I had prepared to perfection. "If Godard could make that picture with a one-hundred-thousand-dollar budget that went mostly for acting talent, think what we can do here if we don't have a payroll for performers," Claude went on breathlessly.

He was referring to Godard's *Breathless*, the cinematic smash of the year. But Godard had made other films with similar success—and a budget that could have been paid out of 20th Century-Fox's petty-cash drawer. Godard disdained the big cranes, the batteries of klieg lights, and the other cumbersome and very expensive panoply of the Hollywood sound stages. He shot his pictures with a 35-millimeter hand camera sitting in a wheelchair that someone pushed forward for close-ups and pulled back for the master scenes. Other low-budget producers like François Truffaut and Claude Chabrol were doing the same thing.

"Well, what do you say?" Claude asked David. "Shall we make the film?"

The idea grabbed David. He loved the theme, which was about how Collioure had become an inspiration to the painters who had taken refuge there during the war and who continued to return there to paint in its tranquil environs. Few if any of the masters were painting in the bright reds, oranges, and yellows of autumnal foliage that gave birth to the Fauve Period thirty years earlier, although they were still producing their modern works, whether of cubism, surrealism, or whatever, in the stimulating surroundings of this serene fishing village.

For David, movie work was not exactly a new thing. Many years before, when he was only seventeen, he had read Jean Cocteau's novel *Thomas the Imposter* and was so fascinated by it that he wrote a movie script based on the book. As fate would have it, that summer David and a friend were vacationing on the Riviera, and who should be staying at the house next door but Jean Cocteau! David brought the script to him. Cocteau read it and told David it was fabulous. Cocteau went ahead and recruited a producer, a director, and a cameraman to shoot the movie. But then Cocteau suffered a heart attack, and the project went into limbo.

It was during his association with Cocteau that the seeds of art forgery were planted in the back of David's mind. David would sit for hours and watch in admiration as Cocteau painted. But observing Cocteau did not turn David into a forger. What really served as his catalyst was a Picasso painting that David spotted in Cocteau's studio—or, at least, what David thought was one of Pablo's works.

"What a marvelous Picasso," David remarked to Cocteau.

"It is not a Picasso," Cocteau grunted. "I painted it myself. But when Pablo came here visiting one day and saw it, he was so taken aback at how much it looked like his own work that he insisted on signing it."

That episode did not launch David into forgery immediately, but it gave him something to think about.

When David, Claude, and Henri started to shoot their movie, the entire town became absorbed in the production. Townspeople and tourists were on their best behavior because they were being filmed in many of the scenes. The star of the show was an illiterate fisherman who, with his wife, had worked for many years in the anchovy cannery. Then suddenly he discovered he could paint. He quit his job in order to devote himself to the brush and palette. He was gifted, of course, and the very simplicity of the man reflected itself in his paintings, which made his works so unique that tourists went out of their way to buy them.

The movie, though finished, was never distributed. David and I eventually took the film to Rome, where some editing was done on it, but it is still there with a friend who is holding it for us and our friends in Collioure.

Although nothing came of the movie, our experience with its production and the fellowship we enjoyed in Collioure remain with me as unforgettable memories. One of my keenest recollections is that of David behind the camera. I think he fancied himself an Elia Kazan—but Elia Kazan, I can tell you after seeing the rushes, he was not.

While we were in Collioure, the mayor invited David and me to the biggest social function of the year, which was held in the landmark twelfth-century castle in the center of the village. Anybody who was anybody was invited to this affair, which included an exhibition of paintings (none by David, of course, and I don't think any of his fakes had reached this precinct yet). Invitations went to mayors, senators, and other ranking officials of government, as well as many celebrities, such as Salvador Dali and his wife, and Madame Saint-Exupéry, the widow of the famed French aviator and author. David and I were probably invited because we had just produced a movie on the village. That it cost us only two hundred dollars to shoot the film was something that few people were aware of.

The party was very dull. I spent most of the time watching Dali eat. He was stuffing his mouth as if food were going out of style. What struck me most about Dali was his glaring bohemian dress and seemingly aberrant life-style. He came in dirty jeans and dirty loafers, which seemed very out of place in this crowd of well-attired dignitaries.

Meanwhile, Dali's wife was constantly attended by a man who acted very much like a gigolo and who looked remarkably like Dali did when he was much younger. Dali didn't seem to mind in the least bit that the señora was getting all that attention from a man who was his mirror-image. Salvador just kept on eating and eating and eating.

Finally David and I got to meet him, but we found we had no rapport with him after we were introduced. He was in one of his moods—and this one was painted in a surrealistic obnoxiousness.

As unpleasant as Dali seemed, I was even less impressed by Madame Saint-Exupéry. It seems inconceivable that such a sensitive writer as her late husband could have been married to such a flashy woman. What especially turned me off was her appearance. She was wearing a gaudy dress, a ton of makeup, and two carnations in her hair.

We spent many enjoyable moments in Collioure. Just before we left, a humorous episode occurred down by the harbor, which is often the scene of vast treasure hunts in the holds of the ancient Roman and Phoenician ships that have sunk in the port. One day our attention was drawn to a man who was a test pilot for Marcel Dassault, of Sud-Aviation, builders of the supersonic Concorde jet. He was a pilot in the French air force before that— until he flew a jet under a bridge. And that finished his career with the air force.

Now he was in Collioure eager to dive for those priceless treasures. Eager is hardly the word; he was fanatical about it. So much so, we decided to play a trick on him. We obtained an urn that had been made in Hong Kong, chipped it a little bit here, a little bit there, and lowered it into some rocks in the shallower depths of the bay.

Then we had someone bait him with a ruse that a skin diver spotted an urn among those rocks a few days ago but was unable to dislodge the treasure from its resting place. The ex-pilot almost flew into the water as the townspeople and tourists, alerted by the gag, gathered at the waterfront.

Soon, the diver surfaced, the urn held high in one hand. He swam to shore as the crowd applauded and cheered. As he came out of the water, one of those who was in on the hoax shouted, "Is there any treasure inside the urn?"

The ex-pilot turned the pot upside down, and a bottle of Pernod came out into his hand. His face turned red from embarrassment. He knew he had been had, for even if the Romans and Phoenicians had put Pernod in bottles in those times, they certainly didn't put "Printed in Paris" labels on them.

5

TEA ISN'T
ALWAYS A DRINK

I was saddened the day we left Collioure because our stay had been so enjoyable. But our departure in August was a matter of necessity. David had to earn some money, and this Mediterranean resort was not exactly the place to ply his buccaneering craft. Switzerland, decided David, was a very good place to do some business.

Our destination was Lausanne, which was holding one of the biggest art exhibitions of the decade. David could see Swiss francs dancing before his eyes as he savored the prospect of inundating the conclave of dealers with his forgeries.

En route, we stopped at Perpignan and flew to Basel because David had an idea that he also might interest the Beyeler Gallery there in some of his "collection." Of course David didn't have a collection, but he was prepared to produce one overnight if Beyeler expressed an interest.

Unfortunately, Beyeler was out of town, and the people at his gallery were too engrossed in their current exhibit featuring the works of the late Nicholas de Staël.

I had gone to school with De Staël's daughter. Her father had committed suicide years before, while he was still a young man. Because he had died in the ascendancy of his career, there was not an extensive number of his paintings. But what there was of them, the Beyeler Gallery had consistently acquired, thus proving his taste and artistic foresight.

When David saw there was no deal to be made in Basel, he decided to head for Lausanne. I was happy to get away from Basel because it was extremely cold, and the heavy Germanic flavor of the city did not warm me.

We registered at the Hotel Montana, truly an Old World inn in every sense of the word. This is where Queen Victoria Eugénie, granddaughter of England's Queen Victoria and wife of King Alphonso III of Spain, and other royalty, as well as nobility, spent their summers. The Queen also played cards at the Montana.

David and I felt like children among the hotel's guests. We didn't see a single person who looked to be under fifty. Most of the women appeared to be dowagers whose mourning period for their late husbands had long passed and now were living off the estates in a regal manner.

There are no bathrooms in the rooms of the Montana. They are out in the hall. And if you wish to take a bath, you must summon a maid who draws the water for you. I suppose that was all right for most of the guests, since they looked to me like people who had been waited on hand and foot all their lives. The food in the Montana's dining room was simply exquisite. Even plain boiled carrots could excite your taste buds. Yes, the Montana, and indeed all of Lausanne, impressed me as a very special place with very special flavors. I loved it there.

So did David. I have lost count of the number of Marie Laurencins, Picassos, and Van Dongens that he painted in our room in the Montana and then sold to dealers and galleries in the city. This was David's most productive period since I had come to live with him.

What was most significant about Lausanne was that David branched out for the first time in my presence into forging the works of still another master, the celebrated and aging Marc Chagall. It was my idea that David paint Chagalls. I'm certain the thought of forging Chagall's works had occurred to David before I suggested it, but it remained for my pushiness to propel him into what became a full-scale onslaught upon the drawing table, from which Chagalls literally cascaded over the next three years.

I had complete faith that David could turn out Chagalls without any difficulty, and his very first efforts at this discipline in our room at the Montana proved me correct. The drawing was of a quality that could have been passed off to any art dealer or gallery as an original. But David wouldn't chance it.

"Here, Anne-Marie," he said.

I then proceeded to shred the painting, which was a variation on Chagall's work entitled "Spring," showing a goat with a violin and done in gouache and pastel. The original was hanging then, as now, in the Museum of Modern Art in São Paulo, Brazil, a gift of New York's Governor Nelson A. Rockefeller.

While David continued in his effort to master Chagall's style, he also turned out paintings to support us. One of these was a Van Dongen, and I remember this transaction very well, because of an unforgettable experience at the gallery of Henri Rey, who dealt not only in paintings but in antique furniture as well.

Rey's father was a very big estate auctioneer, and many of the pieces that came under his hammer found their way into his son's gallery. It was all very legitimate, of course. Moreover, many of the father's wealthy clients patronized young Henri's gallery and bought his works of art.

The day David and I went to see him with the Van Dongen, Rey took one look and shook his head.

"Just lovely, just lovely," he raptured. "I like that."

And he bought it for seven hundred dollars.

As we were about to leave, Rey carried the painting in its frame and hung it in a prominent place on a wall displaying a number of Renoirs.

David squeezed my arm and drew my attention to what Henri was doing.

"Look," David whispered, trying to suppress laughter, "he is hanging our forgery among the Renoirs. It is in its rightful place because the Renoirs are all fakes, too."

"Are you going to tell him?" I asked.

"I don't have the heart to do that," David said, escorting me out of the gallery.

On the way back to the Montana, David and I visited a glittering exhibit of paintings—all of the most beautiful Cézannes, Monets, Bonnards, Toulouse-Lautrecs, and Picassos were on display. I don't believe any museum in the world ever had as many masterpieces as this exhibit held. All of the works had come from private Swiss collections.

What was of greatest interest to David and me, however, was the collection of about a dozen Chagalls. David studied each painting for great lengths of time, absorbing the way Chagall applied colors and drew shapes, but especially the manner in which he juxtaposed the more or less imaginary figures that are found in so many of his works.

When we left the hall housing the exhibit, David turned to me and said, "I have just earned my master's degree. I am ready to paint Chagalls."

But there was more to it than that. Before David would produce his first Chagall forgery for a sale, he bought still more books in addition to the ones we already owned. David studied these for long periods, always practicing, practicing, practicing. As long as we had stayed in Lausanne, David still did not feel he was ready to turn out a Chagall for profit.

It was in Lausanne that I finally came of age as David's accomplice in forgery. David had just assigned another task to me—to buy frames for his paintings. One afternoon I returned with an armful of frames and began to mount David's "old" masterpieces that he had just painted.

When it came time to slip a Picasso into its frame, my eyes were suddenly blinded by the whiteness on the back side of the drawing.

"David," I exclaimed, "what will happen if someone who buys this painting should take it out of the frame?"

"He will probably put it into a more expensive frame," he said jocularly. But he could see I wasn't smiling.

"What do you mean?" he then asked with concern.

"This is supposed to be a painting that Picasso did about twelve years ago," I said. "Look at the paper. It is brand-new."

David shrugged.

"The paper," I went on, "must be aged."

He looked at me in bewilderment.

"And I know just how to do it," I said.

I quickly went to the stove, brewed a large pot of tea, and brought it to David's drawing table. Then I went for some cotton.

When I was a little girl, I had spilled a cup of tea on my homework paper. After drying it up, it looked like a memento from my mother's schooldays. If it "aged" my homework paper, I reasoned, why not the drawing paper on which David was painting his forgeries?

"You are a genius, *chérie*," David said exultantly after my first test application. He took me in his arms and kissed me.

After that, no painting or drawing that David produced ever bypassed the "aging" process. With experience I could "age" the paper for the precise era of the painting. If, for example, David were doing a work of a decade ago, I would brew the tea weakly, so the paper would be slightly yellowed. But if the masterpiece David was forging was older, say twenty years, I would brew a stronger tea.

Another little detail to which a counterfeiting artist must be constantly alerted is the individual eccentricities of certain artists in the way they sign their names. One painter, for example, may turn out his work in pastel but sign it in crayon. You, as the forger, must carefully note which of the artists are disposed to employ these anomalous mediums in their works. Dealers know, and if you should happen to bring in a forgery, no matter how faithful the work may be to the artist's original painting, and you have slipped up on the signature, you're dead. This, in fact, is a very precise science, for it has come to the point where you must even know in what period an artist began employing this erratic treatment in his drawings and paintings. Someone like Picasso, as a further example, has often done a sketch in pencil and signed it in ink. There is no end to the variations.

But there was an end to our stay in Lausanne. With the dozen sales David made, we were well bankrolled for the trip to our next destination—Italy.

6

SAPONE THE TAILOR—
A PICASSO EXPERT?

It was all business from the moment we arrived in Milan on the Paris-Simplon express and checked into the Cavour Hotel. While David was scouting the galleries of the city, one gallery owner, named Bruno Bergamini, told David that he wasn't in the market for paintings at that time, but he was able to recommend a collector and customer who was always interested in works of art. His name was Arturo Tosi, reputed to be the "Tailor of Italy" and often termed the Pierre Cardin of the square Italian generation. His business cards were engraved in raised type with the legend "The Architect of the Human Body."

"Tosi may not want to buy, but he will certainly look at what you have," said Bergamini, who wasn't always an art dealer. During World War II he was said to have made a fortune selling coal. With his wealth he felt anything was better than anthracite, so he opened a gallery and became Milan's leading *venditore d'arte*.

David had an easy time reaching Tosi, who confirmed what Bergamini had said. Tosi would be more than happy to look at David's offerings. He asked David to come over in the morning.

Not knowing David well, one might wonder what kind of gall he had making an appointment to show paintings when he didn't have even one piece back in our suite in the Cavour. But that's the kind of man David was. He would have the "collection" by morning.

One of the reasons that David's portfolio was empty when we got to Milan was a side trip we had taken to Geneva during our stay in Lausanne. While we were in Geneva, David sold one Van Dongen, one Marie Laurencin, and a few China (India) ink sketches by Picasso (which David penned in our room in a matter of minutes), and sold them to the Galerie Benador, one of the best-known art dealers in Geneva. They paid a neat $2,500 for the lot.

David could have painted more pieces in Lausanne and brought them with us to Milan, but he didn't for another reason— fear that customs officials might ask too many questions about them. Each country of Europe has a different set of rules governing the import and export of paintings, and unless you are familiar with the laws, you can get into a lot of trouble transporting art works over the borders.

After making his appointment with Tosi, David stopped at an art-supply store on the way back to the hotel and stocked up on paper, pencils, pastels, inks, crayons, and watercolors. Tea could be ordered through room service.

David didn't go to work until after we returned from dinner. But no sooner had he started sketching for the Picasso and Marie Laurencin forgeries than he quit cold. He was exhausted after the trip from Lausanne and his rounds of the Milan galleries that morning.

"I am going to bed," David said, yawning. "I can do them after a good night's rest."

I knew David could paint in the morning and probably finish in time to keep his ten o'clock appointment with Tosi. But I had never seen him work under that kind of pressure before. I was mainly concerned that his working under the gun like that might make him a little sloppy.

David arose at six. I was awake then, too, but I hadn't gotten out of bed right away. He sat at his drawing board and thought out loud.

"I think I will give Tosi a treat," he said. "I will paint a Picasso series for the pantsmaker."

David selected three very attractive Picasso subjects—the head of a child, "The Three Graces," and a humoristic scene depicting a monk standing in front of a drunken naked man. The name of the series eludes me, but I know that Picasso had painted up to one hundred variations on each of the subjects. That's very common in Picasso's work, and such a propensity for repetition by an artist only made it that much easier for a forger, such as David. How could anyone—even the most astute Picasso expert—ever keep track of so many similar and familiar paintings?

David produced seven Picassos by 8 A.M. and devoted the next forty-five minutes to a Marie Laurencin. He still hadn't shaved or showered, but he managed to perform those toilet functions long before it was time to leave for his appointment. Meanwhile, there was a revolting development.

From the day I had met David, I became aware of his aversion for food before lunchtime. He never had anything for breakfast, except on rare occasions when he would drink a bottle of beer. This was one of those mornings. I kept a wary eye on David—and it happened. He began to gasp for air. I was terrified.

My mind rushed back to a day in Paris when the same thing had happened. David had barely belted down a few ounces of beer when he began struggling for breath. Then he began burping violently. At first I laughed, then I almost cried when I saw what agony he was suffering. He hurried to a doctor who gave him a double shot of phenobarbital to bring him out of it.

The beer, it seems, will occasionally cause a gastric reaction in David. And on this particular morning when David was about to leave on his mission to the Tailor of Italy, he had another seizure. But, as it turned out, it was only a scare. After only a couple of minutes of troubled breathing, David looked at me, smiled, and said, "I'm all right, *chérie*." And he was off to see Tosi.

Tosi greeted David with a big smile and a vigorous handshake.

"*Signore*," the tailor said to my "husband," "I have a big surprise for you. A friend of mine is visiting from France, and I want you to meet him."

David's knees buckled when he shook hands with Monsieur Sapone, another renowned tailor, who happened to have as one of his principal customers none other than Pablo Picasso.

What sent shock waves through David was his awareness that Sapone was also regarded as an expert on Picasso paintings. His expertise came about because Picasso more often than not paid his tailor not in cash but with his paintings. Sapone is reputed to have more Picassos than anyone—including all the tailors—in the world.

"Well, *signore*," said Tosi after the introductions, "where are the paintings you wish to show me?"

David, who was torn between a desire to run and an impulse to stay and put himself to the test, decided to throw himself upon the mercy of the tailor from France. David opened his portfolio and carefully pulled out the Picassos, one by one. He left the Marie Laurencin for last.

And for once in his perky career as a purveyor of legitimate and forged art works, David decided upon the golden rule of silence. I would suggest his glibness was drained by the heavy optical concentration he was giving to Sapone, as he began examining the paintings.

At first Sapone squinted, and his brows furrowed. Then he seemed to be grinding his teeth in concentration. Finally:

"*Maraviglioso!*" he shouted. "These are the best of Picasso for this period that I have ever seen!"

David is the kind of man willing to let well enough alone, but Sapone evidently was not. He continued to rant and rave about the paintings.

"Look at the continuity of those lines, simply marvelous. This is really Picasso at his best."

Sapone passed judgment on each of the Picassos that David had painted, and his verdict was the same from one to the other.

David pulled the Marie Laurencin out of his portfolio as the very last offering.

"It is very beautiful," praised Sapone, "but I am not an expert on this artist."

The Marie Laurencin was indeed beautiful. It was a watercolor portrait of an angelic-looking girl—and David had given all of forty-five minutes to its creation.

With Sapone's paroxysms of ecstasy still reverberating in Tosi's ears, David knew that the tailor to Italy's square generation was ripe for the kill.

"Quanto costano questi?" Tosi asked.

For a moment the Milanese *sarto* had forgotten he was addressing a Frenchman. But David would have understood the question if it had been spoken in Chinese.

"One million three hundred thousand liras," he replied with a calm befitting a man who had just pulled off the best offensive since Anzio. And Tosi obediently went to his desk and wrote out a check for the amount.

David asked if he could use the phone.

"Chérie," he said quietly, "the deal is made."

He didn't dare give me the details because both Tosi and Sapone are bilingual. He asked me to meet him in fifteen minutes at a café midway between the Piazza del Duomo and the Cavour. In less time than that, I was sitting beside David at a sidewalk table outside the café, and he was telling me all about his big sale.

After lunch, David cashed Signore Tosi's check at the hotel. You should have seen the expression on the cashier's face when David handed him the check. The man almost bowed as he counted out the thousand-lira bills into David's hands. If that sounds like a lot of money, it is only about two thousand dollars. But in Italy it has a great deal more value and can go much further on a shopping spree.

David took me to the Rinascente department store and bought me a suit, shoes, handbags, and a very beautiful set of leather luggage for our future travels.

The next morning we went out and bought a dashshund, which we named Bichou. Then we went back to the hotel, and as we entered our room, David took me in his arms, kissed me, and whispered, "What we need now more than anything else is a honeymoon."

I was flabbergasted. I had never given thought to a honeymoon because I had felt my entire relationship with David had been a continuous bridal promenade. He fulfilled all my desires and needs. It may sound corny, but I regarded him as the perfect man, intellectually, emotionally, and sexually. I never for a moment felt bored with David. We never had a breakdown in communicating with each other. As I said, I thought he was perfect.

And now he was going to take me on a honeymoon. We weren't

even married, legally that is, but we were going off somewhere as if we were. The fact that we didn't have that official certificate had never entered my mind in all the years I lived with David. How many women that you know who have been *legally* wed can look you in the eye and tell you what I have said about my "husband" and our relations? Anyway, he bought me a wedding ring in Milan.

In America Niagara Falls is the honeymooners' paradise; in Europe it is Venice. And, David suggested Venice. The Cavour made reservations for us at the Londra Hotel, and the next morning, with Bichou sitting on my lap, we flew to that remarkable city that has been called the Queen of the Adriatic.

Our reservations at the Londra were for the presidential suite, a marbled penthouse with a fantastic balcony overlooking the Grand Canal. During the days I suffered in bed before my miscarriage in Paris, I had read Ernest Hemingway's *Across the River and into the Trees,* and I came to feel almost as strongly about Venice as the author, although I had never been there.

I found Venice mysterious, quiet, peaceful, and cloaked with a timeless quality. I loved the gondola rides, our visit to the church of St. Marks, and the *scuole*, or guild halls, of San Marco, San Teodor, and San Rocco. David and I spent some wonderful evenings in Harry's Bar and other hangouts immortalized by Hemingway in his book.

After five heavenly days in Venice, we had to say good-bye. David wanted to get to Rome and fulfill the plan he had drawn up in Lausanne for the conquest of Italy, indeed all of Europe. The Eternal City was to be our home base.

7

ARRIVEDERCI, ROMA, AND
I'M PREGNANT AGAIN

I'll never know how they were able to accommodate us at the Michelangelo Hotel, a minute's walk from the Vatican. We had a feeling that we would be turned away from the moment we landed at Leonardo da Vinci Airport. Rome was in an S.R.O. state because it was the beginning of the Ecumenical Council. Our hotel was overflowing with bishops, archbishops, cardinals, and nuns in a sea of black and purple colors. But we got a room.

If were to establish a center of operations in Rome, we would have to find a place of some permanence to live. Hotel rooms are too crammed and too costly. So we went house-hunting the next morning, and a renting agent managed to find us a jewel of an apartment in Rome's hilly suburb of Mount Parioli. It was a dramatic, eye-catching furnished flat with a commodious living room and an alcove containing a comfortable studio bed. What puzzled me was the bawdy house pull-drapes, made of red velvet, that separated the two rooms.

I wasn't puzzled anymore after the first few phone calls. In Rome, and for all I know in all of Italy, they don't disconnect phones or change numbers when a tenant moves out and a new one comes in. One of the first calls was for the *manicure* (manicurist), and one that soon followed was for the *massaggiatrice* (masseuse). Everything was cleared up for me by the doorman, who explained that the former occupant of our apartment was a call girl. She moved out when one of the tenants in the building put the heat on her. He was the chief of police.

The renting agent not only established us in our new apartment but also helped to give our social life in Rome a start. In fact, Luigi Filippo di Mehlem became our very first friend there. Luigi had not always been a renting agent. A descendant of a noble family with blood ties to one of the popes, Luigi was by profession and love a nuclear physicist. But he had a wife who envied the material abundances that her sister, married to a movie producer, was enjoying. So she nagged at Luigi until he quit his meager-paying job with the government and became a real-estate broker.

This was a disastrous venture for Luigi. He got involved in a bad business deal and soon found a horde of creditors pounding on his door. It got so bad for him—with the people he owed money to screaming in one ear and his wife yelling in the other—that Luigi slept in his office. But even there they wouldn't let him alone. It reached a point where the phone started ringing at six in the morning. Luigi finally hit upon a solution. He'd answer the call and say, "If you think this is an office, you are crazy. If you think this is a residence, you are very impolite."

And he'd hang up.

About three months later when David and I were preparing to leave Rome, Luigi was arrested and jailed. The last we heard was that his attorney was planning to plead insanity on his client's behalf.

Everywhere I turned in Rome it seemed that people were abandoning their professional careers for better-paying jobs. Luigi had introduced us to Bruno di Geronimo, who gave up being a lawyer to write movie and television scripts. But Bruno, a fascinating man who introduced David and me to many important people in the movie industry, was always broke.

"They don't pay me every week," Bruno would complain. "They make me wait a year for my money."

I know I haven't spoken yet about David's philanthropic bent. He was always an easy touch. The moment he heard a hard-luck story he was hooked. His hand would go into his pocket and out would come a bighearted loan. And he'd seldom get it back.

But Bruno was different. He not only repaid David but also became one of our dearest friends. Bruno also figured in David's third venture into film activity, which was an idea to adapt Tolstoy's *The Death of Ivan Ilyich* to a movie. Bruno went for the concept and worked long hours with David on the script. Then he began to scout around for a cast. He got as far as picking Enrico Maria Salerno, the Laurence Olivier of Italy, to play the lead. But after that, so many roadblocks cropped up that the project was abandoned.

I don't suppose David was fated to succeed in movie ventures, and that was precisely why he turned his full attention to the business he knew best—painting forgeries.

First came a tour of the galleries to determine what works they were buying. David finally settled upon two likely victims just off the Piazza di Spagna—the Galleria Marlborough and the Medusa. David wanted most of all to do business with the Marlborough, for they were a franchised outpost of the famed Marlborough in London. The prestige of selling to this gallery adds considerably to the credentials of a *courtier en peintures* and is often the only entrée an art dealer needs to deal with other galleries.

The director of the Marlborough in Rome, Bruno Herlitzka, a Hungarian who walked with a stiff leg, was gracious and considerate to David, but it remained for his codirector, Signora Palicale, a very attractive and ebullient cosmopolite, to break the ice for him. She bought a Picasso, a crayon drawing from the Artist and Model Period in the 1950's.

The deal also pleased Herlitzka, who introduced David to the Baroness Maglietta, a colorful and delightful person whose native Russian accent flavored her Italian dialect. Her husband, a civil engineer, deferred to his wife's personality to provide the "lift" in the Maglietta family.

The baroness bought one Van Dongen from the Fauve Period, a Dufy, and several Picasso pastels. These pieces and the one bought by Marlborough itself were the very first that David had created in our apartment in Rome.

After these deals, the Galleria Medusa was easy to sell. They had the privilege of buying David's very first Chagall, which, when compared with the hundreds of pieces that my "husband" painted later on, was very empty so far as subject was concerned. The piece portrayed a little clown and a small donkey flying in a big empty sky. But at least the painting had reflected Chagall's traditional flight of fancy and invention.

Before David took that Chagall to the Medusa, we went out to shop for a frame. We spent hours trying to figure which style was best for Chagall's works and finally discovered rococo was the most ideally suited for blend and dramatization.

After the Chagall, David sold a Braque to the Medusa and gradually we began to accumulate some cash. So we started to live it up a bit. First we bought an Innocenti, which looks like an MG but actually has an Austin engine and a Fiat body, and then we looked for a larger apartment. We found what we liked in the Vigna Clara hills outside of Rome where many ambassadors and diplomats live. Our new apartment had a huge living room, dining room, two nice-sized bedrooms, two bathrooms, a kitchen, accommodations for a maid, and a balcony with a fantastic view of Rome.

There were really two reasons why we moved from the apartment. One, David needed more room to do his painting. Two, I was going to have a baby! Yes, above the many other joys of Venice, I became pregnant there.

Because of what happened to me in Paris after my first pregnancy, David and I decided not to take chances. I went to a gynecologist with offices near the Coliseum, and he put me on once-a-week hormone injections to lessen the danger of another miscarriage. He also told me to rest as much as I could and not move around too much.

On November 22, 1964, David and I celebrated another significant milestone. It was my twenty-first birthday, and that meant emancipation from my parents. Although I had declared my freedom from parental superintendence long before then, I was never free to rest my fears that my mother and father might send the police to bring me home. My birthday observance was dampened somewhat, for that was the day our friend Luigi was arrested and tossed into prison.

In our new apartment, with that beautiful view, David found fresh inspiration to paint. Now he wanted to concentrate on Chagalls, which were still a challenge to him, since he had only sold one. That was done in pastel, and David decided to try his hand with other media.

For the next two weeks David worked resolutely at the drawing board turning out Chagalls in crayon, watercolor, and gouache, and he even experimented boldly in oils. But when he reached that medium, I protested. I didn't want David doing oil paintings. And he knew as well as I, if not better, why he musn't mess with that medium. It is too dangerous. The likelihood of catching a forger of oil paintings is a thousandfold greater than catching one who fakes in the other media.

Oil paintings constitute an artist's major works and are almost always cataloged worldwide. Thus, when a counterfeiter tries to sell a fake oil and the gallery owner or art dealer fails to find it listed in the book, he knows immediately that something is fishy.

Moreover, a major oil painting, like a Chagall, cannot be peddled to just any gallery. How many galleries have sixty thousand dollars to shell out for such a work, which is what an oil by Chagall usually goes for?

Not only is it riskier to sell an oil, it also takes much longer to paint. And it is also rather irritating to have someone in confined quarters like apartments painting in that medium. The smell of the oils, turpentines, and varnishes is stifling. They are also very messy.

David had "practiced" on some twelve renditions of Chagall's works in that two-week period and decided that two of the pieces were good enough to sell. But not in Rome. It wasn't that David didn't believe he could have sold them there, but he didn't feel he should take any more chances with Chagall's works in that city. David was still in the infancy of his career as a forger, and he had not outgrown his apprehensions and fears of getting caught.

Around the time of my birthday, I went to the doctor for my weekly injection and told him that I wanted to accompany David on a flight to Turin in northern Italy. He had learned that the Galleria La Bussola was in the market for paintings.

The doctor assured me that I could make the trip without any risk to my pregnancy. I can't blame the doctor for what happened, for he had no way of knowing that the ancient Alitalia Airlines propeller-driven plane would encounter severe turbulence en route to Turin and that the tossing around we got in the air on that one-hour hop would lead to a crisis that very night.

I had barely shaken the dizziness and nausea after a few hours of rest in our room in the Principe di Piemonte Hotel when I began hemorrhaging. I was terribly frightened, but I managed to restore my calm. My previous experience told me that I was not yet in peril of aborting the baby—I had no cramps or fever, nor did I encounter any discomfort other than the bleeding.

By the next evening I was fully recovered, and I saw no reason why I shouldn't go with David to the Galleria La Bussola. We brought two Picassos, the two Chagalls, and three other paintings in the style of Marie Laurencin, Van Dongen, and Braque.

Though our appointment was with the owner of the gallery, the woman at the door explained that he had been delayed by the premature arrival of the stork at one of the houses in Turin. The gallery owner was also a gynecologist.

When he arrived some forty minutes later, he examined David's handiwork and nodded his head approvingly at each of the pieces.

"I would like to buy them all," he apologized, "but I cannot afford it."

David had asked for 1,500,000 liras for the whole lot.

"I would like to buy one Chagall and one Picasso," the doctor said, picking out the two that he wanted. "How much?"

David suggested 500,000 liras.

"I am sorry," shrugged the doctor, who was very tall, very young, and very good-looking. "All I can pay you is three hundred thousand liras. Would you consider that and something very attractive. . . ."

His voice trailed off as he walked to the wall and pointed to a large oil painting. It was one of a number of paintings hanging in the gallery that were the work of the noted Italian painter Sironi, who had died a short while before. The gallery owner had been a close friend of the painter's and had bought many of his works.

David knew that to turn down a Sironi in Italy is bad manners, especially when it is being offered for a mere 200,000 liras, which was the difference between what he wanted in cash for his two fakes and what the doctor was willing to pay.

"I will take it," David said, although I knew he would much rather have had the additional 200,000 liras. Now David would have to troop off to other galleries to unload the Sironi, and even if he were to sell it at a profit, the time wasted wasn't worth it. David could create many forgeries in that time and sell them for much more.

Of course, if you look at it from the point of view of a swindler, which is what David was after all, he was getting a genuine Sironi and 300,000 liras in exchange for two fabricated paintings. That's a deal hard to beat.

David's uncanny ability to size up a pigeon and read his mind led him to whisper in my ear when the doctor went to write the check, "This bird has his eye on the other Picasso, and his mind is going through the gymnastics of how to approach me."

"Signore Stein," the doctor smiled as he handed David the check, "allow me to help you carry your paintings back to the hotel."

When we reached the hotel, David knew he had the doctor hooked on the Picasso.

"May I buy you and the *signora* a drink?" he asked as we walked into the lobby of the Principe di Piemonte. David nudged me. I turned and looked at him. He gave me a knowing wink.

At the table, talk about the change in the weather was very brief—the approaching winter was sending samplings of icy air swirling down upon Turin from the neighboring snow-covered Alps. The doctor changed the subject almost too precipitately when he said, "There is something about that Picasso in your portfolio that intrigues me . . . and I have the same feeling about the one you sold me. . . ." There was a long pause. "I want to ask you a very important question. . . ."

Again the doctor fell upon a spell of silence, a silence that was deafening, for I could see what was going through David's mind. I was terrified myself, for I knew the implications. But most of all I was aware of the possibly dreadful ramifications.

My heart sank to the floor, for just then the door opened, and two uniformed policemen walked in. They stood by the entrance as if they were waiting for something. Or someone!

Now rushing through my mind were the earlier events of the day. Before David had gone to the Galleria La Bussola, he had called to confirm the appointment he had made the day before from Rome and to announce that he was in Turin. When he phoned, the woman at the gallery had said to him that she had neglected to ask him for credentials. David then told her about his dealings with the Marlborough and the Medusa.

"Oh, if it is the Marlborough," she said to David, "then we will check with them."

David had fretted all day about Marlborough's response to La Bussola. Later, when we were having supper in the hotel dining room, David was a bundle of nerves. All sorts of dreadful thoughts were running through his mind.

"You know, *chérie*," he said at one point, "if Marlborough has discovered that the Picasso they bought is a fake, I am cooked. We do not have a sale here, and maybe there could be trouble."

I was thinking of what David had said now as we sat in the bar with the doctor. I turned a quick eye toward the door. The policemen were still standing there.

Suddenly the doctor started to talk again.

"Now that question I started to ask you, Signore Stein. How much would you take for that second Picasso?"

I let out a sigh and turned my eyes to David. Those Alpine winds were not bearing any relief to him. His forehead was at the dew point of perspiration. But the doctor's last words were like a tonic to David. Not a sudden cure, just a tonic. For when he responded to the doctor, David's broad face may have suddenly been creased in a smile, but his voice was thinned by the strain of the last ten seconds.

"I would like to have the same price as the other," David said haltingly, still struggling to compose himself.

The doctor seemed confused. He pointed out that the other Picasso had been sold in a package with the Chagall, and the two together went for 500,000 liras, notwithstanding the deal worked out with the Sironi oil painting.

"Oh," David blurted, his voice stronger, "I'll let it go for two hundred thousand."

Now the doctor was smiling. He thrust his hand into his pocket for his checkbook and eagerly scribbled out the payment for David. Then he gulped the last drop of his Galliano, rose, bowed politely, bubbled *"grazie,"* tucked the Picasso under his arm, tossed a *"ciao"* at us for good measure, and headed toward the door, almost bowling over the two policemen who were still standing there—for no other reason than that they had wanted to come in out of the cold.

8

CHAGALL TELLS US:
"IT'S A FAKE!"

When the woman from the Bussola called the Galleria Marlborough in Rome, she spoke to none other than Bruno Herlitzka himself, who not only confirmed that David had sold Marlborough a Picasso but recited the sale to the Baroness Maglietta. And then Herlitzka, as I since learned, told the woman in Turin, "I not only recommend Signore Stein but urge you to do business with him. He is a fine, upstanding man."

When you are engaged in the shadowy world of art forgery, you can never be certain that your act of chicanery has been consummated until the moment you present a check to the teller at the bank and collect payment. We knew we were home free when La Bussola's bank in Turin cashed both checks and counted out 500,000 liras into David's eager hands. Then we flew the Alitalia route back to Rome. The plane was just as bad as the one that had brought us to Turin, and the flight itself was just as rough.

Since I was dizzy and nauseous again, I went straight to the doctor, who doubled the dose of my hormone injections. He saw no reason to be overly concerned about the hemorrhaging I experienced in Turin. He emphasized my need to rest.

But there was no rest. In early December David decided that it

51

was time to sell to the art market in Vienna. By this time he had built up a bulging portfolio of Picassos, Chagalls, and Dufy landscapes, and, of course, the Sironi oil that no gallery in Rome wanted to buy.

We took the train to Vienna, and somehow I had the feeling that I was riding on the Orient Express, although I'd never been on it. Winter wasn't far, and the farther north we went, the more snow covered the landscape.

We stayed at the exquisite Sacher Hotel, which rivals the Ritz in Paris and then some. When I went to the lobby newsstand and found my favorite magazine sold out, they sent a page boy all over Vienna to bring back a copy. It was a Sunday, but it made no difference.

We expected to stay awhile, and as on all of our extended visits anywhere, David and I planned to combine business with pleasure. Business came first, and David contacted the Peithner-Feichtenfels Gallery and was asked to come in with his paintings. We went together.

The gallery owner, Mr. Peithner-Feichtenfels, flipped over one of the Chagalls, a winter scene done in pastel, and a Picasso watercolor from the Artist and the Studio Period. He readily agreed to buy both and pay David five thousand dollars. But there was no check this time. Peithner-Feichtenfels invited David and me to lunch with him and his wife, who held an important position with an organization affiliated with the United Nations in Vienna. When the gallery owner arrived at the restaurant, he was carrying a large canvas sack that looked very much like the bags vending-machine operators carry. He handed it to David and said, "Here is the payment for the paintings." It was one of the few times that David received cash outright for his forgeries.

With this sale, David decided that the rest of our stay in Vienna should be devoted to rest and relaxation. Though he had many more paintings, he was still clinging to his credo: Never flood one market with too many fakes. David took me sightseeing and shopping and bought me an adorable white Persian lamb slacks-suit. He also bought me a ring and, in the process, inadvertently entered a business deal.

The jewelry-store owner was a Jewish refugee from Russia who, while batting the breeze with David, asked what his occupation was. He nearly vaulted the counter when he learned that David was an art dealer. The owner rushed into the back of the store and returned with a fairly large oil painting

He wanted to know what David thought of it. The painting depicted a green-faced character, undoubtedly a Jew, holding a Torah. When David looked on the back, he decided the painting had done a lot of traveling because it bore dozens of authenticating government stamps—all of them Russian.

David's adrenalin began to flow like a Niagara torrent.

"*Alors!*" he told himself, "this idiot has one of the greatest masterpieces, and he doesn't realize it."

"When did you get this painting?" David inquired.

"Many years ago," the jeweler replied. "Maybe in 1929 or 1930."

Then he asked whether the painting was worth anything.

"Oh," David replied slowly, stroking his chin, "maybe about a hundred thousand dollars."

"*That much?*" the jeweler gasped. "Why?"

"Because," David said, measuring each word, "this . . . happens . . . to . . . be . . . one . . . of . . . Marc . . . Chagall's . . . earliest . . . works."

Well, wheeler-dealer that David was, he tried to persuade the jeweler to let him take the painting on consignment to have it authenticated and if it was really the real McCoy, to try to sell it. There was nothing below-board in what David was trying to do. This is the way art dealers work with galleries as well as art collectors. David was thinking only about that delirious fee, easily twenty thousand dollars.

But the jeweler was a very distrusting soul.

"I have taken pictures of the painting," he said. "Why don't you take them and do your checking?"

Photos will often serve as well to establish the validity of a painting. In fact, that procedure is followed by most art dealers and galleries. So David took the photos. He planned to show them to someone who should know, but the time was not yet. We were still on our Viennese fun-spree. We went to a Beethoven violin concerto at the Opera House and dined on exquisite Hungarian gourmet dishes at the Pataky Restaurant. We spent many hours sight-seeing in Vienna, and I have wonderful memories of the architectural beauties of the city—the old Parliament build-ing, the Rathaus with the high tower, the Votive Church with its twin towers, the Hofburg Theater, and especially the magnifi-cent neo-Renaissance-styled Opera House.

I was sorry to leave Vienna, but David thought we should move on to new territories—in this instance, Germany. We dropped in on Munich first, and David tried to peddle his paint-ings to several galleries, but they didn't even want to look at them. All they were interested in were works of German Expres-sionism. We left Munich in a hurry and went to Düsseldorf, where it was the same story.

Incidentally, Düsseldorf is not a "Little Paris," as the Germans have been inclined to label it. I am amazed at how little they absorbed from their occupation of my own beautiful capital city. I didn't find the slightest comparison between Paris and Düssel-dorf. It is conceivable the many Allied bombs that were dropped during the war changed the face of the city.

Basel was our next port of call. Again, as on our last visit there, David was looking for Mr. Beyeler, owner of the Beyeler Gallery, who had been out of town during our trip in August. This time we stayed at the Kaiser Ludwig, the same hotel Chagall stayed in during his stops in Basel, and this time Beyeler was there.

Beyeler was impressed with the Braque that David showed him, but he didn't want to pay for it. Beyeler wanted to barter one of Marino Marini's works for it. There's one thing you must be wary of when you consider one of Marini's pieces—avoid taking the little man on the horse. But alack, alas, there is no way out. The only thing Marino Marini sculpts and paints is the little man on the horse.

Incredible as it may sound, Marino Marinis go for plenty. When Beyeler made that offer to David, he knew he could sell it without much difficulty and get at least as much as he could for the Braque, which, after all, was worthless, since David had painted it.

The deal was made.

Meanwhile we were still trying to get rid of that Sironi oil painting, which we had dragged through Italy, Austria, Ger-many, and into Switzerland. David had scouted the galleries in Basel, and no one even wanted to look at it. In desperation David decided to make a side trip to Geneva and try to unload it on the museum. Someone had told him that the curator of this museum was partial to Sironis. In fact, they were preparing an exhibit of Sironi's works. Fortunately, the assistant curator was on duty when David got there, and when he looked at the painting, David thought he detected the man's pupils dilating.

"This is magnificent!" the assistant curator rhapsodized. "It is one of Sironi's best!

"Do you wish to sell this painting?" he asked.

With a question like that, what was David to answer?

"Well," he said, "I don't really want to part with it, but when I see that you have created a place of honor in your museum for Signore Sironi's works, what alternative do I have?"

"How much will you take for the painting?" asked the museum's number-two overseer.

David said he'd be willing to part with the Sironi for a thousand dollars. The price grabbed the assistant curator just right.

"It is a deal," he said.

Then came the hang-up. David wanted to get out of Geneva and back to me in Basel. He asked to be paid in cash. The assistant curator backed off. He didn't have that much money in the house. David was still desperate to unload the Sironi and get out of town.

"Look," he said, "you want this painting, and I want to sell it. How much cash do you have?"

"About three hundred dollars," the man answered.

"All right," David said. "I'll take that as down payment, and you will owe me the rest."

The assistant curator's eyes brightened. He thrust his hand into his pocket, pulled out a wad of Swiss francs, and counted out the equivalent of three hundred dollars.

"When will you return for the balance of the payment?" the assistant curator asked.

"Oh, maybe sometime later this week," David answered on the way out.

David never had the opportunity to go back and collect that seven hundred dollars.

We left Basel two days before Christmas and planned to return very shortly and spend a holiday at nearby San Anton. Before then, however, David wanted to emancipate himself from custody of that Marino Marini painting from the Beyeler Gallery. He knew of dealers in Milan who were partial to the native painters and were likely to buy his stylized work.

David also had concluded that I could probably swing a deal for the Marini by posing as the owner of the painting, as I had done with the architect's collection at the Galerie Maeght in Paris. David reasoned that as a *courtier en peintures* he could not deal effectively with the galleries if he were to meet resistance. The cardinal rule in an art dealer's negotiations is never yield too much ground in bargaining over a work. Since David was anxious to dump the Marini and at the same time was cognizant of the possible resistance he could encounter in some galleries, he didn't want to jeopardize his reputation as a resolute negotiator by making a desperation sale. You'd be amazed at how word gets around in the art community about a dealer who bends on price under pressure and how vulnerable he becomes to other dealers who think they can cut his price, too.

By sending me in the pose of a private collector, a prospective buyer could chew me down on the price, and it wouldn't matter. All that really mattered to David and me was getting rid of the Marino Marini.

We departed Basel with dampened spirits. David wasn't going to make that twenty-thousand-dollar commission he was hoping to realize from the sale of the jeweler's Chagall. All because of the verdict rendered by none other than Chagall himself that the oil painting David was so certain was an original, was not.

David had brought the photos of the work to Franz Meyer, the curator of the Kunstmuseum in Basel, who is Chagall's son-in-law. Meyer promised to send the photos to his father-in-law in France for authentication. About a week or so later, David checked with Meyer.

"Definitely not an original Chagall painting," Meyer said sharply. "My father-in-law said that he never did this work. He says it is an outright fake."

David was devastated. Though Chagall's word was final, David refused to believe that Chagall had not produced that work. Well, then, why wouldn't the master acknowledge the painting?

"It's very simple," David told me. "This undoubtedly is a piece Chagall painted when he was still a young man living in Russia. More than likely it was done before he had established a reputation for himself. Probably he didn't even sell the painting but gave it away to a friend."

As David went on to explain, many of today's masters—as well as many of the famed painters of the past—give away their early works or sell them for a pittance, only to find years later after achieving greatness that their old, forgotten paintings were crawling out of the woodwork like termites and being sold for fantastic prices. No matter who the artist, he resents the idea that collectors, art dealers, and galleries can profit handsomely with a work on which he himself made little or no money.

Indignation, then, will often prompt a master to deny the painting as his. When that happens, the value of the work plummets like a security on the stock exchange after the company has gone into bankruptcy.

David was so sickened by the episode at the Kunstmuseum that he never notified the jeweler about Chagall's verdict. After building up his hopes as he had, David didn't have the heart to tell the old merchant that his painting was adjudged worthless.

9

LOST!

We were off now to Stuttgart by train, where I was to catch the morning flight to Milan and sell the Marino Marini. I was to fly on to Vienna, rendezvous with David, and from there proceed together to San Anton for our Christmas holiday.

We arrived in Stuttgart late at night and took a room in a hotel. The weather was cold and clear when we went to bed. When we awakened the following morning, which was the day before Christmas, we were startled by the sight of so much snow. It was a near-blizzard.

David phoned the airport, and we learned to our surprise that though incoming flights had been canceled, planes were still taking off.

We went by taxi to the airport with the Marino Marini wrapped in several protective layers of heavy brown paper. Extreme care had to be exercised in handling this work because it was a *toile marouflée*, an oil done on paper and later pasted on canvas. An artist will often paint on paper when he is planning to use it as a model for sculpting. As a rule, he doesn't consider selling the painting. But art dealers often come into possession of such oils done on paper and mount the works on canvas themselves just to sell them.

The flight to Milan on a Lufthansa Electra was far more comfortable than my other recent hops. In just an hour the weather underwent a splendid transformation. The sun was shining on Milan, and it was warm and pleasant. The city was as beautiful as it had been on my previous trip with David.

Though Milan was bathed in sunlight, customs officials at the airport examined me under a dark cloud of suspicion. It was my first troublesome encounter with border officials. The brown package I was carrying was the focus of their attention.

"What is in that?" one of the agents asked.

"A painting," I replied, trying to give as little information as I could get away with.

"Who painted it?" he wanted to know.

"A friend of mine," I answered. Oh, boy, I said to myself. If they ask to look at it and see Marino Marini's name on it, his "friend" will be in some fix.

"How much did you pay for it?" the man persisted.

"I didn't pay anything for it," I replied with a straight face. It was the truth, after all, wasn't it? But then I said, "It's a Christmas gift that I am taking to someone."

Now a cold chill went up my back.

"Please open the painting," the customs official ordered.

I unwrapped it, and while the agents examined the work, I held my breath. They studied it long and with much deliberation. But not with great care, because they never bothered to look at the signature!

"Eh," the man who had been questioning me said with disdain, "it is not bad. It is not very professional, but it should make your friend a nice Christmas present."

My experience with customs should have told me things weren't going to go right for me in Milan. I was carrying a small suitcase with just a few garments and personal toilet articles for the trip. But I didn't want to lug the bag on my rounds of the galleries and went to the railroad station to check it in a locker. There had been a bomb scare in the station, however, and the police were examining everyone's luggage.

I had nothing to hide, and I wanted to open my suitcase for examination. But the key—I had left it in another bag that was with David.

"You can break the lock open," I suggested to the policeman.

He didn't find that was necessary, although I wished he had. How would *I* open the suitcase later when I would need a change of clothes or makeup?

"Just assure me that you are not carrying any bombs in it," the policeman said.

When I gave him my word that I wasn't concealing explosives, I was allowed to check the suitcase, and off I went to sell the Marino Marini.

My instructions from David were to show the painting to three particular dealers, two of whom he was certain would be at least mildly interested, and the third one definitely interested. The whole idea was to get the highest price.

David had sized up the situation correctly. The first two dealers just shook their heads when they looked at the painting. They didn't want it. Then I went to the third one. I had no way of knowing when I went into the gallery that the owner had just returned from Basel himself and had seen my Marino Marini hanging in the Beyeler Gallery. Nor did I have the foggiest notion that he had wanted the painting in the worst way but was unable to bargain down the price.

Now what do you think his reaction was when I unwrapped the painting and he saw that it was the very one that had gotten away from him? That he would make an offer to buy it? Wrong.

"Where did you get it?" he asked sharply.

I told him a friend had asked me to sell it.

"Do you have a bill of sale?" he demanded.

I didn't have such proof.

"Do you have a consignment receipt?"

Nor that either.

Then he dropped the bomb on me that the police had thought was in the railroad station. He told me about his trip to Basel.

"This is very suspicious," he said. His voice was domineering, arrogant. "I think I had better call the authorities."

I was terrified. I had to think fast. I knew what trouble I was in. That painting could not have crossed the border into Italy in the few days since he had seen it hanging in the Beyeler Gallery in Switzerland unless it had been smuggled into the country. True, loosely speaking, it hadn't been. Customs officials had examined it and allowed me to bring it into Milan. But I had misrepresented the painting. Had I confessed to the truth, then the work would have first been submitted to the Italian Fine Arts Commission, which would take at least a week to give it clearance. What was I going to do?

My first impulse was to grab the Marino Marini and run. Or just run and the heck with the painting. It wasn't worth the price of arrest. But I did some fast thinking.

"Wait a minute, please," I implored the gallery owner. "Do not get so excited. I am not a criminal. I will prove that I am telling the truth. I want you to hold the painting, and I will get in touch with my friend for the consignment order. And that will also give you time to check with the Beyeler Gallery and determine whether this in fact is the painting you saw hanging there."

The suggestion seemed to please him. He went to his office, and while my heart was still pounding out of fear that he might yet call the authorities, he returned with a signed receipt for the painting.

"Here"—and he smiled for the first time—"take this. It shows that I have your painting. I will expect you to bring me the consignment order or the bill of sale. And meanwhile I will check this out with Beyeler. I hope you have told me the truth for your sake."

I was never so glad to get out of a place in my life, and I couldn't wait to put all the distance I could between myself and that man. I jumped into a cab, still muttering curses at David, who should have known better than to send me on such a mission without the proper papers, as well as a warning about the possible pitfalls. One of the insights into the business that David had failed to provide me was the practice of gallery owners traveling to galleries in other countries. Now I had learned about it from a frightening, firsthand experience.

I wanted to go to the railroad station and pick up my suitcase, but I was afraid that I was being followed. I had the driver head in one direction, then another, and only then toward my destination. When I took my bag out of the locker, I still had the feeling I was being shadowed. I didn't trust that gallery owner.

I took another cab, and after I had the driver change direction several times, I told him to take me to the airport. It was 6:30 in the evening when I arrived at the Alitalia ticket counter. Well, here we go again. My favorite airline. I wonder if Alitalia has the roller-coaster concessions at Coney Island, too?

I asked the clerk for a ticket on the next flight to Vienna.

"Sorry," he said, "no planes are taking off for Vienna. They are snowed in, and we cannot land there."

There was no way to reach David. I knew that he was still en route from Stuttgart to Vienna and would not arrive at the hotel where we were to meet for several hours yet.

I worked out some hasty cerebral calculations on alternate routes to Vienna.

"All right," I said, "give me a ticket to Munich." I was thinking that once I reached Munich, I could catch a fast train and be in Vienna in three hours.

"Sorry, there are no seats left on the flight to Munich," the man said.

I thought of Frankfort, a big rail center, and how I could take an overnight train trip to Vienna. David would not be too concerned if I didn't arrive until morning, although he had given me specific orders to take an evening flight out of Milan. He could call the airport and put his mind at ease when he found out that incoming flights had been canceled. In fact, all he'd have to do was look at the snow coming down, and he'd know why I wasn't there.

I'll go to Frankfort, I told myself, and phone David from there.

"Sorry," the man said monotonously, "we have no flights to Frankfort."

I was exasperated.

"Well, do you have any flights at all to anyplace in Germany?" I asked indignantly. The simplest solution, of course, was to stay in a Milan hotel for the night and catch a plane to Vienna in the morning, when the airport would most likely be open. But I wasn't about to take that chance—not when I would be in the proximity of that gallery owner.

"The only thing we have is a flight to Stuttgart," the ticket agent said, "and that plane leaves in five minutes."

I was dumbfounded. "I left Stuttgart this morning," I said, "and no planes were landing because of the storm."

The man raised his eyebrows.

"Well," he sighed, "I am telling you we have a flight to Stuttgart, and we have a seat for you. Do you want it?"

I knew there was no way the plane could land in Stuttgart, and suddenly I had it all figured out. The flight would be diverted for a landing in Frankfort, where I had wanted to go in the third place.

"I'll take the ticket," I said.

I have not been too laudatory in my comments about Alitalia's European service because I haven't found anything nice to say about it thus far. But on the flight to Stuttgart it was like a different airline flying the route. True, we were aboard a Caravelle, which is a French plane, but even the service left nothing to be desired. Well, almost nothing.

I bought my ticket very close to flight time, and by the time I arrived at the terminal's boarding ramp, the gate was closed. The plane was taxiing to the runway, but an Alitalia steward came to my rescue. He phoned to stop the plane, and then took me out in a car to board the flight.

Once in the air, another steward who saw how fatigued I was escorted me across the aisle to a row of three-across seats that were unoccupied.

"You can stretch out here," he told me.

I was grateful to him. I was exhausted, physically and emotionally, and the opportunity to stretch out and relax was like an elixir. I lost track of time in midflight, and I was more asleep than awake when a voice over the loudspeaker suddenly aroused me. It was the captain:

"Because of a snowstorm, we will be unable to complete our flight to Stuttgart. We will land at Frankfort instead, where you will be given accommodations."

I smiled.

I smiled again when we landed. The plane to Munich that had no seat for me had also been diverted by the storm and was on the apron next to ours.

Alitalia's service continued to be great. They provided buses that took us to a hotel in Frankfort. Everything was so wonderful until I went for my suitcase. It wasn't on the bus. Nor on the plane. The steward who had driven me out to the plane had forgotten to put it aboard!

So there I was in Frankfort with only the clothes I was wearing. Not even a toothbrush, though I didn't mind that very much, since I wasn't taking advantage of Alitalia's hospitality at the hotel anyway. I planned to catch the train for Vienna.

I went to phone David from the hotel lobby, but since it was Christmas Eve, the telephone operators were not working that night. I was frantic. I couldn't place a call to Vienna or even send a telegram.

I hurried out of the hotel and walked around the corner to the railroad station. A train was leaving for Vienna in five minutes, and they had a sleeping compartment for me.

As I climbed into bed, a terrible thought crossed my mind. What if David called the galleries in Milan and learned from the owner who kept the Marino Marini what had happened? What would David think when he was told that I had left the painting there to obtain proof of ownership? Most likely he would assume I was still in Milan trying to work the problem out. He might very well decide to go there and find me.

I had a very restless night. The thought of finding David gone by the time I reached Vienna terrified me. I finally fell asleep out of sheer exhaustion.

We arrived in Vienna early the next morning, and the city was buried under a blanket of white. It looked just like Vienna should on Christmas Day. I rushed to a phone at the station and called the hotel where I was to meet David. More devastating news. David wasn't there, nor had he left any message for me. Worse, he wasn't even registered there.

I couldn't imagine why David had done this to me. He had promised that if the hotel didn't have a room for him, he would leave a message saying where I could find him. Had David gone to Milan? I wondered. More than ever, now I believed he had.

But I decided on a long shot—the Sacher. Since we had stayed at that hotel before, I reasoned, David might very well have gone there again. I summoned a cab.

Just as we pulled up in front of the Sacher, who should I see standing there, waiting for a taxi, but David—and with the rest of our luggage! I rushed up and threw my arms around him. David kissed me.

"What happened to you?" he wanted to know. I was so thrilled and excited to see him that I didn't want to talk about it just then.

"I'll explain later," I told him.

Then I looked at our luggage, and it suddenly dawned on me to ask David, "Where were you going?"

"Why, to Milan, to find you," he said.

David was impatient for an explanation about my trouble in Milan, and I had to tell him.

"That complicates the situation," he frowned. "If we go to San Anton, they might trace us there."

The last thing David wanted was an encounter with the authorities, but I just couldn't see how it was possible to pick up our trail after all the double-backing and city-hopping I had done to cover my tracks. But I deferred to his judgment.

"We have got to go somewhere far from here where it will be much safer," David said. He decided that Frankfort might be a provident haven, for a while at least. We went to the airport, and it was truly Christmas Day. There were no scheduled flights.

Luckily, however, a Turkish airline plane bound from Ankara to Frankfort had made a stopover in Vienna, and they had two seats for us. It was about 2 P.M. when we left Vienna behind, and not too long afterward an announcement that was familiar to my ears was made on the loudspeaker. Frankfort was locked in by a snowstorm, and the captain was plotting the course to an alternative landing site. We weren't told where that would be, and some minutes later when the captain came out of the pilot's compartment and walked down the aisle past us, David took his sleeve.

"What are the odds that we will land in Milan?" David asked.

The captain shook his head. "We do not have enough fuel for such a flight," he answered.

David looked at me. We were both smiling.

As it turned out, we landed in Amsterdam—a good place to be on Christmas night or during any night when you consider our fears of arrest.

Though I was feeble from all that traveling and yearning for a good night's sleep in that comfortable bed in our room at the Hilton, my elation at being reunited with David gave me strength to go on for a few more hours. We went to the bar in the lobby for a drink, then to dinner in a delightful Indonesian restaurant. The manager of the Hilton even opened the drugstore for me so that I could buy a toothbrush and comb.

We stayed in Amsterdam for two days. We did nothing but eat and drink in the best restaurants and nightclubs, but I was unimpressed with the nightlife there. It is vulgar and common and reminds me of the atmosphere in Hamburg's red-light district. During our two days in Amsterdam, however, I began to feel a new closeness to David, and I think he felt closer to me. The separation, my hair-raising adventure in Milan, the tribulations of travel I experienced over half the continent of Europe, and then that accidental reunion outside the Sacher seemed to carry David and me to a new plateau of understanding and togetherness. I think David put it best when he cuddled up to me in bed on our last night in Amsterdam and whispered, "If after all that has happened to us in the past few days and we are still together, it must be God's will. We were meant to be together."

10

DAVID AND
THE PICKPOCKET

Although we could have stayed on in Amsterdam for rest and relaxation as we had planned to do in San Anton, David and I decided we had had enough of leisure. When you think about it, even when David was painting and selling to galleries, we never worked that much. David always made it a point to take me to dinner, the theater, opera, concerts, and other enjoyable places. Ours had not been a hard life in the time we had been together. Hectic, yes, but not hard.

The wheels in David's mind were turning again. He was thinking ahead to more painting and more sales. What country, what city, should we travel to next?

David decided on London, for he had been there before and had made many friends whom he yearned to see again. But more than that—there are so many galleries, and the art market is very active there.

When I went off to Milan, our little dachshund Bichou had stayed with David. Now on the flight to London, Bichou must have made a good impression on the KLM people, for they allowed her to sit on my lap instead of taking a pet's customary place in the luggage compartment. When we landed in London some forty-five minutes later, however, the English customs officials didn't take kindly to our dog. They appeared to be very put out that Bichou had stepped on English soil without having gone through quarantine.

"Pick up that dog!" one customs man shouted.

"How did you get that dog into the passenger terminal?" another blustery agent demanded.

David tried to explain that the airline had allowed him to ride in the plane with us.

"Impossible," the first immigration officer shouted. He phoned the airline. Couldn't have happened, a KLM spokesman told the caller.

Anyway, British customs solved the problem very officiously. They took Bichou in a KLM car to the airport kennel and placed him in quarantine. And to make certain he got there, a motorcycle policeman escorted the car to the kennel.

The customs men never even looked at our suitcases. We could have been smuggling fifty pounds of heroin and another fifty of cocaine or hashish, and they never would have discovered it. Bichou had bothered them so much that they completely neglected to inspect our luggage.

We took a cab to a hotel on Curzon Street in the heart of London. From the moment of our arrival to the moment we left, I could not get over how I was unable to orient myself to the city. I found it impossible to get around. I'm certain it's the way the streets are laid out.

While we were in Amsterdam, we had met an Englishman who practiced law in London. After David and I settled down, we looked him up. His office was a small, dingy cubbyhole in the Soho district. He represented some of the lesser lights in the entertainment world. The lawyer was about David's age and very bright, but he lacked ambition and vigor to move ahead. He seemed satisfied to drift in the backwaters of the legal profession with his little band of show-business performers. He was also very dull.

He invited us to a New Year's Eve party in a private house. The party and the people that he invited were as unexciting as the barrister. The guest list consisted of a number of his roommates. There were twelve roommates in all, and each had a girl friend who more or less lived in that flat. But you never knew whose girl friend was whose from one week to the next because they switched them so often.

A few days after the party, the lawyer told us that one of his clients, a manager of topless dancers, was marrying a belly dancer. He recruited David and me as witnesses for the ceremony at Borough Hall. The next day they were off on their honeymoon to Turkey, where the girl had an engagement to shake her belly in a nightclub in Istanbul.

Despite all this social activity, David was paying a good deal of attention to business. His first goal was to find one of his old cronies. Rowen came from a very respectable London family. His father was a well-known *maître d'hôtel* at one of the city's leading hotels. His brothers and sisters were all upstanding citizens. But Rowen was a pickpocket.

That isn't as bad as it sounds, for as I learned, a pickpocket in London is a special breed of badman. When he is arrested, his friends take care of his wife and children while he is in jail. His friends are also pickpockets.

David had no other thought in looking Rowen up than to renew an old friendship. He had known Rowen from the time David had gone to school in London as a teen-ager.

David had no idea where Rowen was living, and it was pure luck that he got together with him one day while we were walking through Soho's streets. All at once I heard someone shouting, "I say there, David, old boy. . . ." The next thing I knew, David and this man had their arms around each other. Rowen had recognized David.

I found Rowen a very likable man. He had had little formal education, spoke with a thick cockney accent, and was not exactly the kind of person you'd expect to find in the British Foreign Service. But Rowen had many charming qualities. He was handsome, he had a wonderful sense of humor, and, what I judge to be a most admirable trait, he had a deep sense of loyalty toward his friends. In the time I had known David, he had introduced me to countless numbers of people involved or allied with the art world. Most, if not all, were cultured and well educated. It wasn't often we ran into down-to-earth people like Rowen.

Rowen took David and me to his home in the Whitechapel district (where Charlie Chaplin came from). His wife made coffee for us. Since I was pregnant, and since Rowen's wife had two small children, most of our talk was about kids. After that we saw Rowen and his family almost every day. Occasionally we went out together.

About a week after our association with Rowen had begun, David decided there was a more respectable vocation for Rowen than pickpocketing, which had been his only means of livelihood. At the beginning, Rowen had asked David what kind of work he was in. David told him he was selling paintings to art galleries, but nothing more. Now after a week had passed, he decided to tell Rowen the whole story. David thought that Rowen might be the perfect person to sell our forged paintings to the august London galleries.

Rowen found it very exciting that David was painting Picassos, Chagalls, and works of other renowned artists, although Rowen had never heard of them. He had never picked their pockets. Rowen began to regard David with new admiration and respect, perhaps because David was involved in illegal activity. But I'll never forget the way Rowen put it when he heard what David was doing.

"Why, this is fabulous, old boy," Rowen trilled. "You are a crook with class."

As David viewed him, Rowen was a good prospect as a salesman for the forged works. More than that, Rowen could be David's safety valve in his illicit activity. After what had happened in Milan, David had become a little gun-shy. He was beginning to feel that he was not as invulnerable as he thought he was. Moreover, he was aware of the limitations that bound him in his illegal ventures. David spoke with a French accent. He had a distinctive face that greatly resembled Orson Welles'. In short, he was easily recognizable and identifiable. He was concerned about that because he realized that the more forged paintings he sold himself, the better known he would become and the greater his chances would be of getting caught. Since I had a French accent, David reasoned, I wasn't any less vulnerable than he. But if he could recruit Rowen into the "organization," then David and I wouldn't have to expose ourselves as often at the art galleries.

Rowen was carried away with the idea, when David suggested that he sell forged paintings to London's leading galleries. It pre-sented him with an opportunity of making more money with one sale than he could make in a month picking pockets. But Rowen also thought that by having an entrée to the galleries he could pick the pockets of the wealthy patrons simultaneously.

Rowen was disappointed, however, when David told him that it would be some time before he could make his first sale.

"Why?" he asked in bewilderment.

"Because," David answered, "you just can't take one of my paintings, walk into an art gallery, and try to sell it."

"Why not?" Rowen inquired, his face still masked by puzzlement.

"Because you have to know a few things about works of art and about painters," David explained. "If you pose as a collector who is trying to sell some of his valuable possessions, you need to know a great deal about your paintings. And there is another thing. . . ."

"What's that?" Rowen asked as he detected a hesitancy in David.

"You have to improve your diction," David said.

"My what?" asked Rowen as if he couldn't believe his ears.

"Your diction," David repeated. "That cockney accent will not get you past the doormen at the galleries."

Rowen wanted to know what had to be done. David told him. Then began a long period of training for Rowen. With David coaching him, Rowen absorbed information about painters and paintings that David intended to paint and sell at London galleries.

It was like a scene from *Pygmalion*.

Meanwhile, David and I had tired of our hotel-life existence and moved into an apartment in Dolphin Square. It was there that David unpacked his art supplies and began to paint. His first creation was a Chagall watercolor and gouache depicting a familiar variation of the donkey, flying ballerina, and fiddler floating in the sky. Then he sketched a Van Dongen in pastels which represented the master's style from the Fauve Period. Both works would command good prices.

David's cram-course for Rowen was geared toward a thorough knowledge about Van Dongens and Chagalls and biographical data about the artists, since the pickpocket's first assignment was to sell these masters' works. The day finally came when David decided that Rowen was ready to meet his first challenge in the staid art world of London.

"Take these paintings to the O'Hanna Gallery," David instructed Rowen. He told him whom to see at the gallery, for David had phoned earlier and made an appointment to show the Van Dongen and Chagall.

David and I went with Rowen as far as the corner of Old Bond Street and then let him go the rest of the way himself. Meanwhile, we went into the pub at the corner to wait for Rowen.

A half hour later, Rowen walked into the pub, a broad smile on his face. He was empty-handed. When David saw him without the paintings, he smiled, too. When he saw the check in Rowen's hand, he ordered a glass of stout for Rowen, another round of stout for himself, and another ale for me.

It was time to celebrate, for Rowen had sold the two pieces for a substantial three thousand pounds, or about $8,000.

"How did you do it?" asked David as he sipped his stout.

Rowen told the story. He went into the gallery, looked up Mr. O'Hanna, with whom David had made the appointment for Rowen, and showed him the two paintings. O'Hanna was at once impressed with what he saw.

"All I did was to tell Mr. O'Hanna what you had said to me— that I wanted to sell them for three thousand pounds."

"Did he give you any argument?" interrupted David.

"Down the hatch," said Rowen as he drank the stout in one fell swoop. "No lip from the bloke. Took them like he was robbing me blind."

Rowen turned to the waiter and ordered another stout. Then he looked at David.

"I didn't do bloody bad, did I?" he asked.

David patted him on the back.

"Now you owe me three hundred pounds," Rowen laughed. "With that kind of money I can keep out of people's pockets for at least a month."

"I'm going to pay you immediately," David told Rowen.

"You'd better," Rowen came back. "The bloody check is made out in my name."

We walked to a Barclay's around the corner, where Rowen pre-sented the check to the teller and received the three thousand pounds. David paid him his commission, pocketed the rest, and we all went back to the pub for a hearty lunch.

David didn't paint anything else in the month that we spent in London, and Rowen was never employed again to sell a forged painting. David had felt the sale to O'Hanna was a good killing, and he didn't want to press his luck.

In all our travels in Europe, David and I needed only to show our identification cards issued by the French government. Passports aren't required to enter and leave European cities except those in Iron Curtain countries. Neither David nor I had a passport. But for quite some time now, David had been talking about going to America. He didn't particularly care whether it was North or South America, just so long as it was one of the countries of the western hemisphere.

We were seated in a pub in Soho one night with Rowen and reliving his adventures as a pickpocket, and he was telling of how he often plucked traveler's checks out of people's pockets. That was always a problem, he complained. In order to convert the checks to cash, Rowen related, he would be compelled to take a quick flight abroad to Paris, Berlin, Amsterdam, Brussels, or some other such nearby capital, where getting cash for the stolen checks was a lesser risk than chancing arrest in London, where authorities were more likely to know about the theft.

Rowen was telling us how he established different identities for himself. David was intrigued. He wanted to know how Rowen did it.

"You simply walk into Borough Hall and apply for a traveler's card. You can go in as often as you want and apply for one under as many names as you wish. They don't ask you for a birth certificate or any other proof. They take your word for whatever you tell them."

There was only one thing you had to be careful about, Rowen told David. That was to make certain you told the people who issued the identification cards at Borough Hall that you were born on British soil. You had to be especially careful to tell them that if you happened to speak with a French accent, as David and I did.

And, of course, this put a hell of an idea in David's head. All at once he could envision his dream of a lifetime coming true— going to America to launch his career as an art forger on a *grande échelle.*

The next day, David and I went to a photographer and posed for standard-sized passport photos. A few hours later, David headed for Borough Hall to get identification cards for himself and me. A while later, David returned home with the cards. I signed my card, and he took it back to Borough Hall, where it was stamped with the official British seal.

We were now in a position to travel as British subjects any- where in Europe except for the Iron Curtain countries, as well as the British dominions. That, of course, included Canada, which David had decided was our ultimate destination. How we would enter the United States itself had not yet been resolved in our minds, but we were more than aware of the traditional reciprocity existing between the immigration authorities of the two countries that enabled citizens to cross from either border without showing passports or having to submit to any lengthy inspection pro- cedures.

David wanted to begin painting forgeries on a vast scale, far beyond the rather limited production of his operations thus far.

As I said earlier, it is virtually impossible to flood the art mar- ket of any city in Europe with a plethora of fakes. If you want to avoid getting caught, the method that succeeds is the one David had employed—sell one, two, or three in a city, then get out, go somewhere else, sell a few there, then go to another place.

It is extremely difficult to get away with selling forgeries by the dozen in any one city on the Continent unless you have a very extensive and sophisticated organization with many cour- tiers. But when you operate as David did, literally a one-man organization with an occasional assist by me, the marketplace is greatly restricted.

We had known of another art forger who refused to work modestly. He did his works on a *grande échelle,* and he never showed his face in the galleries. His courtiers did his dirty work. But the venture failed.

I'm referring to Claude Schecroun, who was a master at forg- ing Léger and Miró. Actually, Schecroun had studied with Léger and adapted the famed artist's style so expertly that he could produce a Léger charcoal faster than the master himself.

When Schecroun decided to mass-produce his forgeries of those two noted artists, he established an organization that comprised a number of courtiers, of whom three happened to have been themselves quite reputable citizens of France. One of them was an employee of the Galerie Maeght in Paris, and the other two were nephews of Marcel Dassault, the owner of Sud-Aviation, builders of the Concorde. The venture met with incredible success but only for a month.

They were careless and very indiscreet. They launched their venture in Switzerland, and the headiness of their first quick sales—and large income—prompted them to pursue a form of exhibitionism that no forger should ever undertake. They held lavish parties in their hotel suites, invited young people like themselves to their bashes, and attracted an inordinate amount of attention. As a result, gallery owners began asking questions, and fairly soon they began making inquiries to the Galerie Maeght in Paris. What the gallery owners and collectors in Switzerland who had been buying from this free-swinging group of courtiers wanted to know was why the Galerie Maeght was putting on such splashes in Lausanne, Basel, Geneva, and Zurich. No such thing, said the director of the Galerie Maeght. Never heard of those people. They're phonies. We never sent anyone to Switzerland with Léger and Miró paintings. And before very long, Claude Schecroun and his three cohorts were in the clutches of the law. They went to trial, were convicted, and were sent to prison.

So you can see why it isn't advisable to conduct art forgery on such a large scale in Europe, or to make yourself too conspicuous when you are involved in an illicit venture. In fact, it isn't advisable to pursue that routine in the Americas or anywhere. David had thought it was, and that is why I am writing this book now. Because even David was fooled after he embarked on his career in the United States.

11

DAVID SELLS THREE PICASSOS—
IN BARCELONA!

We spent our last two days in London shopping and packing for Spain, where David planned to pass off a few last paintings before we availed ourselves of Uncle Sam's hospitality. I couldn't wait for the moment we boarded the British European Airways propjet for Madrid, because the January weather in London had chilled me to the bone and gotten me down.

Madrid was a different world for David and me. It was our first venture onto Spanish soil, and the bright warm sun was a welcome sight. We stayed at the luxurious Castilliana Hilton, but after a couple of days we decided it was too expensive. The rates at the Plaza Hotel were more reasonable, but we didn't stay there long either, because after a round of Madrid's galleries, David knew he wasn't going to make any sales. The art dealers weren't in a buying stance.

But on his tour through Madrid, David learned that the dealers in Barcelona were looking for works of art, and we readied ourselves for the trip north. We packed at a leisurely pace, for we were enjoying what Madrid had to offer: the sights such as Paseo del Prado, with its parks, ponds, fountains, and monuments; the afternoon siestas that emphasize the city's casual life-style; the late, lazy dining in candlelit restaurants; and the delicious sips of sweet-tasting anisette at the sidewalk cafés.

The train ride to Barcelona was an experience I'd like to forget. It took something like twelve hours, and the ride on those rickety old sleeping cars was miserable. I still felt the vibrations of the trip when we checked into the Crystal, a hotel that seemed to cater to a clientele composed mostly of the diplomatic corps posted in Barcelona. David and I were in our element again.

David didn't wait long to look up a woman who had been recommended to him in Madrid. She was a *courtière* with excellent contacts at all of Barcelona's galleries. The woman was from Spanish nobility, and her husband taught art at the University of Fine Arts in Barcelona. The couple enjoyed the distinction of having Miró as the best man at their wedding.

Her first question to David was, "What paintings do you have in your collection?"

Knowing that Picassos were in greatest demand in Barcelona, David let the lady know that he had about a half dozen of Picasso's works, but mentioned that he also had a few Chagalls, Dufys, Van Dongens, and Marie Laurencins. Would she like to see them? Yes, she did. David promised to return with the paintings.

What David didn't—and couldn't—tell her was that he had only three small paintings in his portfolio, that he would have to sit down and create the rest. Actually, David didn't even have paper to draw on. Nor did we have tea, which I would need to age the paper. On his way back to the hotel, David picked up these important supplies, and when he entered our room, he announced, "We've got to go to work. Brew some tea, Anne-Marie."

In a couple of hours I had "aged" enough paper to enable David to begin mass-producing the masters' works in his own hand.

David often had to establish a mood when he painted. To do any one artist's work, he had to sort of psych himself into the belief that he was that particular painter. But it never took him long to build up the emotional surge he required to paint the forgery. And once in that mood, David had to continue producing paintings by that artist—he just couldn't switch, say, from a Picasso to a Chagall, then to a Van Dongen. He had to complete the number of drawings he planned to make of that artist, then take a rest, build up a mood that would put him in the frame of mind that he was someone else, then begin painting again.

Perhaps because we were in Barcelona, which is Picasso country, David fell into his Picasso mood first. I remember it was
about five o'clock in the afternoon that David began to produce
his first Picasso, a pen-and-ink variation of "The Three Graces."
It took him exactly fifteen minutes to complete the drawing.
Then he turned to me, lighted a cigarette, and asked, "How do
you like it?"

"I like it," I replied after studying the finished sketch.

I think I should again stress my role as a critic of David's
paintings and other works he produced. I was never easy on him.
As I learned more and more about the different artists whom
David was forging, I acquired more expertise in judging his imitations. I never allowed my love for David to interfere with my
honesty in appraising his work. If it had the slightest imperfec-
tion, I would tell David, and he would direct me to destroy the
painting. In judging David's Picassos, I was especially hard on
him, because I have a deep fondness and respect for this master's
creativity.

David's second and third Picassos that evening were also pen-
and-ink sketches playing on the same "Three Graces" theme.
Working under great pressure, since he had promised to show the
courtière his "collection" the next morning, David was at his best.
He did his finest forgeries under the gun. On the other hand,
when there was no pressure on him—no "deadlines" to meet—his
work seemed to lack perfection. That was because he would take
the opportunity then to experiment with new techniques to master the style of the master he was forging. In effect, David was
striving for perfection.

David then knocked off three more Picassos in a row before we
went to dinner in the hotel restaurant. Two were crayon drawings from the Artist and the Studio series and the other a wash in
the same theme. All six were acceptable representations of Picasso's works, and I was as confident as David was that the galleries
would buy them.

After dinner we returned to our room, and David put on his
Chagall hat. In a few minutes he was stroking the brush across
the paper as though Chagall himself were guiding his hand. It
was always a delight to watch David create his Chagalls, for it is
without exception a challenge to forge any work of this master,

whose artistry, whose play with color combinations, and whose application and buildup of hues are so distinctive and so difficult to imitate.

It took David just two hours to complete this Chagall, a typical watercolor-and-pastel painting depicting the characteristic donkey, fiddler, rooster, and the rest of the subjects that the master invariably incorporated in each of his works.

It was a good night's output. David was now prepared to meet the *courtière* in the morning and make the rounds of the galleries to unload his fakes. He didn't have to paint the Dufy, Van Dongen, or Marie Laurencin, because David had one of each left over in the portfolio that he had brought from London.

Just as we had anticipated, the *courtière* liked all of the paintings and assured David that she would have no difficulty selling them.

"I know a collector who will buy them in a minute," she said. "How much do you want for them?"

"Let us say fifteen thousand dollars," David replied with a straight face and a lump in his stomach. He was sort of reaching for the moon.

"That sounds like a nice price," the *courtière* said, obviously pleased with the prospect of earning some three thousand in commissions.

Then she took us to lunch.

In late afternoon she phoned David at the hotel.

"He is wild about them," she said, referring to her client, the collector. "He wants to see you in the morning to discuss the price."

Next day, the *courtière* took David to meet Rene Metras, a wealthy Spanish industrialist, who promptly shocked his visitors.

"I just got off the phone with Paris," he said. "I spoke with Louise Leiris, and I'm afraid I have some bad news for you."

David was petrified. What had Madame Leiris told Metras? After all, she was an associate of D. H. Kahnweiler—Picasso's exclusive dealer!

"I have learned that Picasso has made so many of the 'Three Graces' drawings that they are not worth as much as you have asked for them," Metras told David and the *courtière*.

I need not tell you what relief swept through David. The

words were like a Bach concerto. He had expected to hear the worst—a declaration that the paintings were fakes. Of course, when you look back on that episode, you must realize that it was an impossibility for Madame Leiris to have judged the three Picassos on the telephone. But when you're involved in a clandestine venture such as the one David was in, the aura of fear is constant, and the slightest hitch or suggestion of suspicion cast in your direction tends to be unnerving.

David was still in shock as the collector spoke on. David wasn't catching every word, but he did finally grasp the most significant part of the dialogue—when money was mentioned.

". . . I am advised," David heard the man saying, "to pay you no more than ten thousand dollars for the paintings that I want, the Picassos and the Chagall. You understand, of course, that I am offering you full price for the Chagall. But as far as the Picassos go, I must abide by the advice and guidance of Madame Leiris."

David swallowed hard. He was getting ten thousand dollars for the Picassos and the Chagall, and he still had the Van Dongen, Dufy, and Marie Laurencin to sell elsewhere for at least three thousand. Not bad, that ten thousand dollars, for a few hours of work.

It was noon when David returned, and the look on his face was enough to tell me that he had made a very good sale. He bounced into the room, took me into his embrace, and kissed me.

"How much did you get?" I asked.

I collapsed on the bed when he took the roll of pesetas out of his pocket. On the way back from the collector's house, David had stopped at the bank and cashed the check.

David and I were now prepared to leave Barcelona. The sale gave us enough capital to finance our dream trip to the New World. It was time to return to Madrid and ready ourselves for that journey.

We decided to fly to Madrid and avoid that terrible train ride. But it was a mistake. The Iberian Airlines plane was a relic. I think it had been left over from the pioneering days of aviation. And the weather was bad. But what really drove me nearly out of my mind on that bumpy hour-and-a-half flight was the elderly passenger seated next to me. I didn't mind the earplugs he was

wearing, and I envied him for that because the noise of the pro-
peller engines was deafening. But what especially upset me was
that this man was so terrified that he had begun to run his prayer
beads through his hands. And every time we hit an air pocket, he
would make his cross.

We returned to the Plaza Hotel, and now we rented a suite. I
recovered quickly from the ordeal of the flight, but the next
morning I realized the damage that had been done. I had hemor-
rhaged during the night. I roused David, who called the desk
clerk for a doctor.

In minutes the doctor came, examined me, and listened to my
recital about the previous bleeding I had experienced in October
and the miscarriage I had suffered in Paris. He administered the
same treatment that the gynecologist in Rome had prescribed—a
hormone injection. He also advised me to take plenty of bed rest.
I followed his orders only for a few hours. By then I felt well
enough to get on my feet. I dressed, and David took me to lunch.

Our visit to Spain also produced other dividends. David and I
met two lovely vacationing American couples who would figure
prominently in our future after we arrived in the United States.
One of the couples was Lee and Minne Katz from Mahopac, New
York, whom we met in the lobby of the Plaza. Lee, a national
salesman for Empire Kosher Poultry, was good-natured and
down-to-earth, and I liked him very much. His wife was quiet,
soft-spoken, and very pleasant. We lunched with them a few
times, and when they learned about our plan to come to the
United States, they both insisted that we get in touch with them
when we arrived. We promised that we would.

The other couple was Sam and June Rosenfeld, of Oceanside,
Long Island, whom we met in Seville at the Alfonso XII Hotel,
where we stayed after we left Madrid en route to Canada. We
went to Seville four days after David's fabulous sale to Señor
Metras. We had no other reason in going to Seville than to enjoy
a brief vacation in that beautiful city with its pleasant climate,
and it was there that we mapped our itinerary for Canada.

After three glorious days in Seville, which we spent eating,
drinking, visiting such historic sights as the broad Alameda de
Hercules with its two Roman pillars bearing statues of Julius Cae-
sar and Hercules, and its gardens and rows of trees, David and I

boarded a small plane with the Rosenfelds and flew to Lisbon. Sam and June were on their way to New York, and David and I were bound for Montreal. The Rosenfelds, who had already met the vaccination requirements, got away almost immediately. David and I heard that we had to remain in Lisbon for three days in order to have smallpox shots before we could fly to Montreal. David called the desk clerk and asked him to send a doctor to our room to do the honors. It was as simple as that.

12

HERE WE COME,
AMERICA

The day after we were vaccinated, David and I left the hotel with our baggage and went to the airport by cab. David had made reservations on a Canadian-Pacific Airlines flight. We took off in a DC-9 just before noon with a planeload of Portuguese emigrants, who were on their way to settlements in Canada where they hoped to find that better way of life that millions of Europe's emigrants had discovered before them in the New World.

The flight was smooth, but I wasn't comfortable after the first hour. Any flight longer than that makes me fidgety, and in my pregnant condition the hours of being glued to my seat made me increasingly unsettled and tired.

We had had excellent weather all across the Atlantic, but when we landed in Montreal, the skies were a dismal gray, and the ground was covered with snow. It was a dreary scene, and though I was relieved that the long and tiring air journey was at an end, I felt very depressed.

I didn't like the little I saw of Montreal on the cab ride from the airport to the Sheraton Hotel, but I was buoyed by the knowledge that we were not going to remain in Canada for long. Our primary goal was to cross the border into the United States and head for our ultimate destination—New York City.

The big problem that confronted us was how. We were aware that most border crossings were a breeze, but we also knew that here and there immigration officials would pull spot checks. Suppose we were singled out for a thoroughgoing examination? Without passports we'd be dead. But that was the chance we'd have to take. Taking chances was nothing new to David and me.

Although I am French and a lot of French is spoken in Montreal, I didn't find the language very comforting to hear, nor too readily understandable. It sounded more like peasant French.

David still had a good deal of the money left from his sale in Barcelona, but he was anxious to add to our finances before we crossed into the United States. And since David knew of only one way to make money, he decided to whip up a few forgeries. Our room in the Sheraton, however, was hardly the place to create Picassos, Marie Laurencins, or Dufys—the intrusion of chambermaids was distracting—so after a few days we moved into a small furnished studio apartment that provided the privacy David required to produce his imitations of the masters. The routine was much the same as it had always been. We went shopping for drawing paper and paints—and tea and cotton. Then David went to work.

His creations consisted of four Picassos, four Chagalls, two Dufys, three Van Dongens, one Marie Laurencin, and one Braque. David worked at a leisurely pace turning out these paintings. There was no particular rush, since we were still giving a great deal of thought to the strategy we would employ in crossing into the United States. We wanted to make certain our entry was foolproof.

It wasn't until our second week in Montreal that David finally finished with his portfolio of forgeries and decided to canvass the city's galleries for likely victims. He spent several days visiting different galleries, and by then he had a fairly good idea what artists' works were in demand, and they happened to be exactly the paintings that he had done in our apartment.

David narrowed his field to two galleries that had expressed a particular interest in his "collection." One was Stern, the other Aldington. He visited them in that order. He sold one Chagall to

Stern and one to Aldington, for a cool total of seven thousand dollars.

David returned to our apartment to drop off his portfolio and then headed for the bank to cash the two checks. For the first time, David didn't have to present an identification to the teller, as he invariably had to do everywhere in Europe. That was because David had opened a bank account in Montreal—and that was the gimmick that would be our "passport" into the United States. It worked this way:

If by chance David and I were singled out for a thorough check at the border, David would present his bank passbook. Of course his account would have a balance, which would convince the immigration people that we had roots in Canada and apparent intentions of returning.

Shortly before nine o'clock on the night of March 31, 1965, David and I boarded the pullman car of the New York Central's Montreal–New York overnighter. A short while after we had left Canada's largest city behind us, David and I were sitting in the dining car for a late evening snack. Suddenly we were approached by an immigration official. He stopped at our table and asked us in French where we were heading.

"*Nous allons passer un mois en Floride,*" David replied. This was the time of year when Canadians were still spending winter vacations in the Sunshine State, and David had prepared that answer.

Who was I? the man asked.

"*Mon nom est Anne-Marie Stein,*" I replied.

There could be no doubt in his mind that I was David Stein's wife—not with my bulging stomach.

Nor could there have been reason to suspect that either David or I was not a Canadian. We had both listened to the provincial French that Montrealers speak and had practiced for hours to perfect the accent. When we answered the official's questions and spoke that Montreal French so fluently, we had him convinced that we were indeed genuine Montrealers. He never even asked to see our bankbook.

As the man left our table and headed up the aisle to check on other passengers, David and I stared into each other's eyes in silence, but we read the relief each of us felt from having passed the immigration check. We were home free at last!

My first glimpse of the United States was through the window of our pullman car. At the first glint of daylight, I caught sight of the pleasant rolling hills of the Hudson Valley and the farms with their spacious barns and healthy-looking livestock meandering on the wintry landscape. It was exactly as I had pictured America. I had seen so many movies and television shows portraying such similar scenes that I had come to expect it. Even my glimpse of small towns and villages with their picturesque homes and narrow streets was like scenes out of *Father Knows Best* or an Andy Hardy adventure, which invariably depicted the suburbs and country as the epitome of clean, comfortable, and casual living. I had the impression that the whole of America might be like that, but it didn't take more than a few days to realize that this panorama etched in my mind was as fraudulent as one of David's Chagalls. When I saw firsthand the slums of Harlem, the ghettos of Jersey City, and the many seamy streets of New York and other cities across the country, I realized that the tableau of ugliness I had seen in *West Side Story* was not just a stage setting but actually a very real portrait of a large part of the United States.

Even in my disappointment, though, I was thrilled to be in this new land. I felt that I had found a home at last and that no matter how much ugliness I had seen, I wanted to remain here. It might sound corny to say that I looked upon the United States as a land of opportunity, but that's the way I felt—and so did David.

Since David and I always booked the best accommodations whenever we could afford them, we decided not to deny ourselves that luxury when we arrived in New York.

"The Pierre Hotel," David directed the cabbie who picked us up at Grand Central Station.

Not many hours after we had settled down in our suite, David phoned Lee and Minne Katz in Lake Mahopac to let them know that we had arrived. The next day they drove down in their Impala convertible and talked us into checking out of the Pierre and coming to stay with them. With the rates we were paying for our accommodations—and we didn't even have a view of Fifth

Avenue or a side street (our window overlooked a dreary inside courtyard)—we were more than eager to accept their invitation.

The Katzes' home was very pleasant and comfortable, situated on a hilltop with a commanding view of the lake. But we spent very little time at the house, for Lee and Minne brought us down to the city almost every day for apartment hunting. Our search finally led to Rego Park in the "suburban" borough of Queens and to a one-bedroom, third-floor furnished apartment in Caroline Gardens on Sixtieth Road, right off the world's "longest parking lot," the Long Island Expressway.

Not many days after David and I moved into the apartment, we learned that we had just missed sharing tenancy in the building with one of America's more notorious citizens, Joseph Bonano, Jr., the son of Mafia overlord Joseph "Joe Bananas" Bonano, who had taken refuge there to escape bullets that were flying in the gangland war between his father's mobsters and the rival Gallo brothers gang. If you read Gay Talese's *Honor Thy Father*, you will recall that young Joe had been holed up in a Queens apartment house. That was our building.

Now at last, with peace, tranquillity, and good home-cooking, David was ready to launch his career as a forger in the United States. First, of course, he had to determine what works of art were in demand on the market. This he did by visiting the city's many galleries. He was like a child turned loose in Macy's toy department, for New York has more galleries than any city in the world, except possibly Paris.

It didn't take David long to find his first customer. She was a lovely, middle-aged woman named Janine Wolkenberg, who was the art buyer for Brentano's bookstores. David introduced himself to Mrs. Wolkenberg as an art broker and informed her that he had a vast collection of works by the modern masters. He reeled off the names of Chagall, Picasso, Dufy, Van Dongen, Marie Laurencin, and the others whom David had come to imitate so well. He also mentioned that he had a formidable collection of drawings by Jean Cocteau.

"At the moment," Mrs. Wolkenberg advised David, "I am very much on the lookout for Cocteau. If you say you have so many of his drawings, why don't you let me see them?"

"May I bring them in tomorrow?" David asked.

The answer was Yes. This was so typical of David. He didn't have a single Cocteau in his portfolio, but that was no handicap. If Brentano's was in the market for Cocteaus, David would supply them.

David didn't rush into production. We had a casual dinner, and sometime in the early evening he went to the drafting table that he had bought a few days earlier. It was the first time in his career that David had bothered to acquire what for most artists is an indispensable piece of equipment. Until now he had done most of his forgeries on the coffee tables of hotel rooms or kitchen tables of our furnished rooms and apartments.

The drafting table seemed to give David incredible inspiration and speed. No sooner had he sat down than he began to rip off one Cocteau after another with a rapidity that astounded me. In five minutes David had shaped a linear profile of Orpheus, and five minutes later he had finished a profile of Orpheus' wife, Eurydice. Though there is said to be the meaning of darkness in the root of Orpheus' name, the drawings that David was producing now were bringing a bright new light into our lives.

As David reached the midpoint of that night's production, he turned, handed me another finished drawing, and broke his long silence.

"Here is another hundred-dollar bill," David said in a gleeful voice.

Long before midnight, David had put his crayons away. He had finished his Cocteau kick. He had produced forty drawings in less than four hours, and he was ready to return to Brentano's in the morning for his first sale in the United States.

Mrs. Wolkenberg flipped over David's "collection." She studied the first dozen or so drawings with a careful eye, then skimmed through the rest of the medley of Cocteaus.

"How much do you want for them?" she asked.

"One hundred each," David replied matter-of-factly.

"Good," Mrs. Wolkenberg said. "That was exactly what I had in mind to offer you. Now, let me see . . . forty drawings at one hundred dollars each . . . that will be four thousand dollars. I will put the payment through for you."

David was sailing on a cloud now, but Mrs. Wolkenberg didn't let him float away. She wanted David to know that she had a little side business in art separate from her position with Brentano's. She was selling drawings and paintings that she was acquiring in her rounds to private collectors. These works were not what her employer stocked, because Brentano's was not a gallery but principally a bookstore chain. Art was only a minor part of the firm's business, and it was sold only as an accommodation to its customers.

"Perhaps you can let me look at your collection of the other artists sometime," Mrs. Wolkenberg said to David. "I may be able to find clients who are interested in some of the paintings."

David said he would be delighted to show her what he had.

"I'll be in touch with you very soon," he promised.

Before he left, Mrs. Wolkenberg told him that she might very well want to buy a painting or two from David's collection for herself.

"Do you have any interesting Chagalls?" she asked.

"You will love what I have," David assured her.

His response quickly led to an invitation to Mrs. Wolkenberg's apartment in Manhattan's West Fifties.

"Why don't you come over tomorrow evening," Mrs. Wolkenberg suggested. "And bring your wife. My husband will be home, and I'm certain we'll enjoy each other's company."

When David arrived home, I knew from the glow on his face that he had succeeded with the sale. Another clue was that he wasn't carrying the bulky portfolio that he had taken with him that morning.

"*Quel pays fantastique!*" David exclaimed.

When he told me that he had sold the forty Cocteaus for four thousand dollars, I couldn't agree more—this indeed was a fantastic country.

The next evening, David and I went to the Wolkenbergs' apartment and spent a memorable time with this wonderful couple. The evening was made even more momentous because David had brought along a Chagall version of his *Quelle Vie, Quel Plaisir* (What Life, What Pleasure), which Mrs. Wolkenberg fell in love with at first sight and readily agreed to pay David four thousand dollars for the painting, done in gouache.

The sale aside, I found the Wolkenbergs a wonderful, intellectual couple without phony airs. Mr. Wolkenberg was a sculptor engaged in reproducing works of other artists. The sculptures he duplicated, and labeled as such, were sold at Brentano's among other places.

Mrs. Wolkenberg sympathized with me when I told her about the difficulties I was encountering in keeping house in my seventh month of pregnancy. She immediately found a solution.

"Let me lend you my maid to help out," she suggested. "She can come over once a week, and it will take a big load off your back."

The suggestion appealed to me, and I agreed to hire Susy, a very portly black woman, to do my household chores every Friday. In time, Mrs. Wolkenberg would be helpful in other ways.

But what counted most now, besides the friendship that had developed with the Wolkenbergs, was the eight thousand dollars that David had made in two days. It was enough to make him believe that if he acquired sufficient capital as a crook, he might even go straight. David was thinking that if he were able to save enough money, he could become a dealer in legitimate works of art and abandon his illicit painting activity.

David preparing to paint a Chagall, with daughter Cecilia looking on.
Photo courtesy of *The Daily Telegraph Magazine*.

Anne-Marie preparing paper for painting, according to tea ritual.
Photo courtesy of *The Daily Telegraph Magazine.*

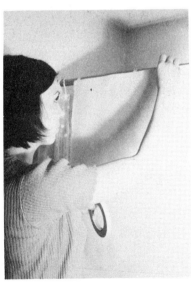

Anne-Marie hanging paper to dry
after application of tea. Photo
courtesy of *The Daily Telegraph
Magazine.*

The start of a fake Chagall. Photo
courtesy of *The Daily Telegraph
Magazine.*

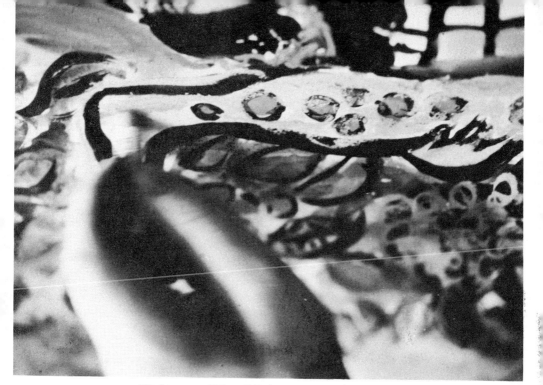

Working on a "Chagall." Photo courtesy of
The Daily Telegraph Magazine.

The finished product. Photo
courtesy of *The Daily
Telegraph Magazine.*

Chagall, painted by David for cover of the London *Telegraph*'s Sunday magazine. Photo courtesy of *The Daily Telegraph Magazine*.

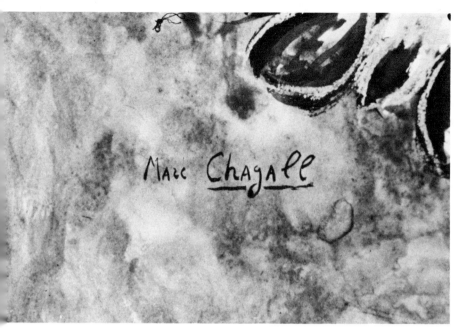

Marc Chagall's signature: the finishing touch. Photo
courtesy of *The Daily Telegraph Magazine*.

A fake Chagall that ended up in Korvette's art gallery.

Fake Chagall sold to A. Lublin.

Fake Chagall sold to L. D. Cohen.

Fake Chagall sold to Irving Yamet.

Fake Chagall sold to Irving Yamet.

In the style of Chagall. Painted in the Tombs prison, 1968. Photo courtesy
of Stefan Congrat-Butlar.

In the style of Picasso. Painted in Toulouse during incarceration, 1971.
(*Property of Mr. and Mrs. Leonard L. Loewinthan of New York.*) Photo
courtesy of Stefan Congrat-Butlar.

In the style of Picasso. Painted in the Tombs during David's incarceration, 1968. Photo courtesy of Stefan Congrat-Butlar.

Fake Picasso.

In the style of Degas. Painted in Paris, 1969, in the Prison of
Fresnes. Photo courtesy of *The Daily Telegraph Magazine*.

In the style of Villon. Painted in the Prison of Fresnes, 1969.
Photo courtesy of *The Daily Telegraph Magazine*.

Anne-Marie in London, January 1965.

Bernard Colson, David, and Anne-Marie
at the Copacabana, New York,
May 1965.

Photograph of David, reproduced in the Palm Beach *Pictorial*
after he made the highest bid for Gladys Robinson's painting
at benefit sale for the Red Cross. With David are
(*left to right*) Lady Gladys Garthwaite, Mrs. Shirley Segal,
and Gregg Juarez, owner of gallery where sale was held.

David, with Mrs. George
Garvin and Mrs. Gladys
Robinson, at party brunch in
Palm Beach. Photo courtesy of
Mort Kaye Studios, Inc.

Palm Beach opening of the Galerie Trianon, February 1966, with (*left to right*)
David, Anne-Marie, Mr. and Mrs. William Findlay, Jr., Mrs. Gladys Robinson, and
William Findlay, Sr. Photo courtesy of Mort Kaye Studios, Inc.

Palm Beach opening of the
Galerie Trianon: George
Schraft, with a friend of
William Randolph Hearst
III, and the manager of
Palm Beach Bonwit Teller.
Photo courtesy of Mort Kaye
Studios, Inc.

Palm Beach opening of the Galerie
Trianon: David and Mrs. Nathan B.
Spingold. Photo courtesy of Bob
Davidoff.

Palm Beach opening of the Galerie
Trianon: David and Mrs. L. Carlebach.
Photo courtesy of Mort Kaye Studios, Inc.

Anne-Marie and Miss Sylvia Hahlo dining at The Colony Hotel in Palm Beach. Photo courtesy of Mort Kaye Studios, Inc.

Anne-Marie and eight-month-old Cecilia in Palm Beach. Photo courtesy of Mort Kaye Studios, Inc.

David and William Findlay, Jr., displaying some of the Findlay's paintings just recovered from the FBI. Photo courtesy of Mort Kaye Studios, Inc.

David in front of the Palm Beach Gallery.

Anne-Marie Stein with her three children, Cecilia, Frédéric, and Jason in their New Jersey home, 1973. Photo courtesy of Stefan Congrat-Butlar.

Wright/Hepburn/Webster Gallery

205 East 60th Street, New York, N. Y. 10022

MASTER FORGER
DAVID STEIN

Presents

| BRAQUE | KLEE | MIRO |
| CHAGALL | MATISSE | PICASSO |

PREVIEW: 5 p.m. to 8 p.m.
Tuesday, September 15th

September 16th through October 3rd

Invitation to one of David's New York exhibitions.

13

THE MAN
FROM MAEGHT

During one of our frequent social get-togethers with Minne and
Lee Katz, David began thinking out loud about opening his own
art dealership. His thoughts were woven more out of fancy than
the thinnest thread of reality, for such a venture would require
an enormous amount of capital. David certainly had no prospects
of raising that kind of money in the immediate future no matter
how many fakes he sold. Any art dealer worth his gouache must
have a substantial collection of paintings—not forgeries, but legitimate works whose cost runs into the many thousands of dollars. Even to start such a business on a shoestring, as David
imagined he could—by putting many of his own fakes into
stock—he would still need a generous assortment of genuine
paintings to bestow on the dealership an aura and substance of
legitimacy.

Despite the seeming improbability that David could swing
that deal so soon after his arrival in the United States, Lee took a
totally different view. He was confident that David could become
an art dealer almost anytime he pleased.

"I know a couple of people who could help you start," Lee told
David one night at dinner.

Lee explained who the people were—Nat Kramer and his son
Lawrence, partners in the accounting firm of Kramer and Berger,

with offices on the fifty-seventh floor of the Empire State Building.

"I'm going to get you together with Nat and Larry," Lee told David. "They're wizards in finance. If anyone can tell you how to set up a business and make money in it, they're the ones who can do it."

The meeting with Nat and Larry Kramer took place in the latter part of April in their suite in what was still the world's tallest building. It didn't take much to convince the Kramers that a dealer in art works reaps huge profits. This was a pleasant surprsie to the accountants, who had never handled a client from the world of art. The bulk of their accounts were in the world of commerce.

Before the meeting was over, the Kramers were so enthusiastic about the glowing portrait of potential success and profits that David had glibly painted for them that they offered one of their offices in the Empire State Building for his art dealership.

David was astonished at the sudden turn of events that were now about to propel him into a business of his own which just an hour ago seemed to be years beyond his grasp. The Kramers' expression of faith and confidence in David's proposal was matched by their generosity, for the office they singled out for the business was to be rented for a mere $150 a month—a bargain-basement figure for such a lofty address. In addition, the Kramers consented to take care of the legal work involved in setting up a corporation for David's new enterprise.

The most perplexing aspect of forming the corporate setup proved to be in the name. It took David and me hours of careful thought and consideration in picking a name that conveyed a French feeling to the business. We finally decided on Concorde Gallery. But when the name was submitted in the incorporation papers to the State Secretary in Albany, we were dismayed to learn that we couldn't use it. The Concord Hotel up in the Catskills had already adopted that name for its own art gallery. Janine Wolkenberg finally came to the rescue by suggesting Galerie Trianon—after one of the palaces at Versailles—and that solved the problem of a name.

David moved swiftly to start the business. First he transferred the dozen or so fake paintings stored in our apartment to his new office. The collection consisted mostly of Chagalls and Picassos. Then he went out and bought an assortment of legitimate drawings, lithographs, and etchings by Picasso, Braque, Matisse, Rouault, Pascin, and Calder, among others. He paid about four thousand dollars for this stock, but it gave the gallery the nucleus that David needed to fulfill his ultimate goal—to sell only legitimate works of art. But for the time being and until he could acquire the capital necessary for buying legitimate works of art, David would run the business with a combined inventory of inexpensive forgeries and bona fide works.

Not many days after he had opened the dealership, David got one of his really big breaks. He'd gone to visit the Graphis Gallery in Greenwich Village and who should be on the floor but Bernard Colson, one of the top representatives of the Galerie Maeght in Paris. The introduction was made by Robert Horn, the owner of Graphis.

Colson had just arrived in New York with a portfolio of graphics introducing a line of Maeght's new publications. Colson was at once won over by David's charm and manner, but most of all the man from Maeght was thrilled to find a fellow Frenchman in a strange city. Colson could not resist David's invitation to dinner in our apartment that night. But first he had to keep commitments at several other galleries. David agreed to meet Colson at the end of the day in mid-Manhattan and bring him out to Queens.

I remember that day vividly. David phoned me just after he left Graphis and told me to prepare dinner for our distinguished visitor.

"And in the name of the Eiffel Tower," he urged me, "hide those Chagalls."

He was referring to his forgeries that we had framed and hung in the apartment because we liked them so much. I also made certain to put David's drafting table and art supplies in the closet.

I prepared a typical French dinner for our guest—roast leg of lamb stuffed with garlic, *flageolets*, and a tasty French salad which I served with Beaujolais. If there is any truth to the old saw that the way to a man's heart is through his stomach, I am confident that Monsieur Colson was won over by our dinner.

After that night and during the next six weeks until Colson returned to Paris, we enjoyed each other's company almost every night and on many weekends in Southampton in a bungalow which we had rented from a motel on the bay. What was most significant about our friendship with Colson was the deep interest he had taken in David and his art dealership. Colson felt that David, as a newcomer to this country, might find the road to success long and tedious unless he had someone well known in the art world to open the doors for him in the city's better art galleries.

"I would like to introduce you to some of the dealers and gallery owners in New York," suggested Colson, whose connection with Maeght gave him entrée not only into every gallery in the city but also with the biggest dealers in the country.

Colson took David to literally dozens of galleries and art dealers, and those introductions opened vast opportunities to David, who otherwise would never have been able to meet the important figures in the art world in so short a time. The dealers couldn't help but be impressed with David when the formal presentation was made by someone as influential as the emissary from Maeght.

It wasn't long before David began to reap bountiful dividends from Colson's benefaction. One of the first important sales that David made came quite by accident—after Colson introduced him to Abraham Lublin, owner of one of the country's largest graphic publishing firms.

That introduction led to an invitation to David and me for cocktails at Lublin's apartment on Central Park West. On our way, David and I stopped at Dain & Schiff on Madison Avenue to pick up a Chagall that we had left in the shop for framing. We took the painting in its brown paper wrapping to Lublin's apartment, and it immediately attracted his curiosity.

"What have you got there?" he wanted to know.

"Oh, it's just a little Chagall," David replied.

Would David mind showing it to him, Lublin asked.

David gulped. He turned to me with a quizzical expression. I knew what was going through his mind—suppose Lublin detected that the painting was a fake? How embarrassing, especially since Bernard Colson had brought Lublin and David together. But there was no way out for David. He had to unwrap the painting.

"Oh, it's so adorable," Lublin sighed as he studied the gouache-and-pastel version of a Russian village that David had painted a few nights before while I was listening to Bach's *Brandenburg Concerti* on our stereo.

"How much could I sell it for?" Lublin asked without taking his eyes off the painting.

"You could get six thousand for it without an argument," David replied.

"And how much will you sell it to me for?" Lublin came back, now turning his eyes, first to David and then to me.

"I think you are entitled to make a nice profit on the sale," David said with extravagant diplomacy. "So I could let you have it for, say, four thousand."

"That's a deal!" Lublin said with enthusiasm. Then he turned to his wife and asked if she had the cash to pay David. Mrs. Lublin shook her head.

"I took the money to the bank," she said. Lublin asked David if he'd mind waiting until the next day for payment.

"Not at all," David said, smiling. "I'll drop by your office to-morrow."

Then David turned his attention to me and, still smiling, raised his glass of Pernod in a toast. I returned the gesture with my drink and tried to contain my joy over the ease with which David had unloaded his fake. We had come to the party without any intention of doing business, and we left four thousand dollars richer.

In the days and weeks ahead, David sold a number of his fakes to gallery owners and individuals introduced to him by Colson, but none of the transactions was of any great significance. The forgeries were small pieces, and they brought in a few hundred dollars here, a few hundred there, but nothing more startling than that.

What was startling, however, was David's near sale of a Picasso to Sears, Roebuck & Company for fourteen thousand dollars. Bernard Colson had taken David to Boston to introduce him to the city's gallery owners and art dealers while he himself was there pushing Maeght's lithographs. During dinner in our apartment one night following their return, Colson turned to David and asked, "How would you like to make another trip with me?"

Colson explained that he was going to Chicago to show Maeght graphics to Sears' art buyers.

"You can bring your collection along," Colson told David. "Sears might be interested in buying some of those works."

David looked at me. I could read his eyes. He was going to ask me to come along. Those three days he had been away in Boston had been absolute torture for me. He knew that, and he didn't want me to suffer again. Separations of more than a day from him were unbearable for me. I was now in my ninth month of pregnancy and perilously close to the moment of truth, and I didn't want to be apart from David for even an hour.

"I'll go with you," I said before he got the words out of his mouth.

We flew from LaGuardia Airport on a TWA 707 jet to Chicago's O'Hare Airport, and it was a vast improvement over the domestic carriers that I was accustomed to in Europe. Except for the food. We had taken off at about 9 P.M., and the dinner hour— American style—was over. So the food on that two-hour hop consisted of some very stale sandwiches.

I'm sorry that I was not able to go along with David when he went with Colson to Sears the next evening to attend a birthday party for Vincent Price, who was the art adviser for the giant merchandising firm.

David had brought along his collection of paintings, for in addition to the celebration, David and Colson had been asked to show their portfolios to Price and the Sears executives. Of all the pieces that David had brought with him, only one, a Picasso gouache, of the artist's atelier, appealed to them. David had spent an exorbitant twelve hours painting it in our Rego Park apartment. Every executive—including Vincent Price—raved about the painting.

David was asked how much he wanted for it. His answer: eighteen thousand dollars!

One executive, Harry Sondheim, approached David.

"Look here, Mr. Stein," he said firmly, "I am going to write out the check right here and now. The figure I am going to pay you is fourteen thousand."

Even as he spoke, the Sears official began writing the check.

"I'm sorry," David came back, "I cannot take anything less than eighteen thousand."

Sondheim looked up in astonishment.

"Look," he said with annoyance, "I've made out the check. And I have even signed it. You mean you will not take fourteen thousand for your Picasso?"

"Not a penny less than eighteen," David replied.

"You have got to be kidding," the executive came back.

"I am not kidding," David said in a resolute voice. "That is my price, and I will not back away from it. This is a very special Picasso, and I refuse to part with it for anything less than what I have asked."

His adamancy infuriated Sondheim, who could see that David would not acquiesce to any lesser figure.

"Do you know what he did?" David said to me that night when he came back to our suite in the Sheraton. "He tore up the fourteen-thousand-dollar check and threw it into the wastebasket."

I didn't have to ask David why he muffed an opportunity to make a clear fourteen thousand—his biggest sale ever. I had known David for fourteen months by now, and I understood his thinking. David was convinced that Picasso was good enough to command eighteen thousand, and he was certain he could get that price. Moreover, we had more than ten thousand in our bank account by now, and David, buoyed by his introduction by Colson to some of the most prestigious gallery owners in New York and Boston, had begun to take on some of the characteristics of a riverboat gambler. He was playing for big stakes. His attitude was, "If you're going to cheat them, cheat them big."

And why not? I asked myself. Didn't David have all the aces up his sleeve? Or should I say the Picassos, Chagalls, Dufys, Marie Laurencins, Braques, Van Dongens, and Cocteaus?

After our return from Chicago, nothing of any consequence occurred over the next thirteen days. Then on the night of June 9 I received a call from David.

"I have to meet some business people, and I won't be able to make it for dinner," David said to me. "I will be home late."

I wasn't happy to hear that. I was so close to giving birth that I had desperately wanted David to be with me. During our fifteen months together David had stayed away from me only once before because of "business," other than legitimate trips he had had to take. And I never asked him where he had been that night, because I do not have a suspicious nature. I have always felt that whatever David does, he usually has a good reason for doing it.

But on this night of June 9 I began to feel different. I had lain in bed watching CBS-TV's late show, late-late show, and late-late-late show until 5 A.M. And during those long hours I experienced a new kind of torment. I felt anxiety for David. Could he have been in a car accident? As the hours dragged on and there was no word from him, I approached a point where I thought I was going out of my mind worrying about him.

Then at five o'clock the phone rang.

"*Chérie*," I heard David's voice, "you'll never guess what happened. I was out with these people, and what do you think? We had a flat tire. . . ."

For the first time I felt suspicious of David. The excuse sounded flimsy. Yet I was willing to believe the story—except for one thing. Why couldn't David have phoned me during the last eleven hours and told me that he was tied up on his "business deal"?

I was sitting up in bed, fully awake, when David walked in at 6:30 A.M. He looked at me and snarled, "Don't you start screaming at me. Nothing happened. I was out on business, and what I told you on the phone is the truth—we had a flat tire."

I had no intention of screaming at David, and I don't know where he got the idea that I would—except that I suspected for a very brief moment that perhaps he hadn't been out on "business" after all. My suspicion was heightened when I asked myself why David had become so defensive if he didn't have anything to hide.

Though it was five and a half hours till noon, the rest of the morning for me was a matter of an eleven o'clock appointment with my gynecologist, Dr. Herbert Hall, on the Upper East Side. He was going to give me what ostensibly would be the last checkup before he delivered the baby.

I didn't sleep a wink even after David had gotten home. I was so angry that the moment he plopped into bed beside me, I got up and made myself a cup of coffee. At nine o'clock I shook David awake and reminded him about my doctor's appointment. He got up, dressed, and took me there in a cab.

This was Thursday, June 10.

"If you don't go into labor over the weekend," Dr. Hall told me, "I'll check you into the hospital on Monday and induce labor."

With that assurance, I went into Saks Fifth Avenue, bought myself a thirty-dollar nightgown, and went home to prepare dinner for ten persons. It was Bernard Colson's birthday, and David and I had planned to give him a party.

It was a delightful affair, and the guests very thoughtfully departed by midnight. By then, David and I were friends again. We went to bed, and David fell asleep immediately. But I did not, because I had a backache throughout most of the night, and in the early morning hours I suddenly began to feel contractions.

I roused David out of a deep sleep.

"I'm beginning to have labor pains," I said.

David bolted into a sitting position on the bed, picked up the phone, and called Dr. Hall.

The answering-service operator told David:

"Don't allow her to drink any liquids and take her right to the hospital."

I then packed my valise with my best nightgown and the other paraphernalia I thought a mother-to-be should bring with her, and David took me in a taxi to the Flower and Fifth Avenue Hospital.

A nurse gave me an injection of sodium pentathol just after I was wheeled into the labor room, and I slept soundly until I woke up in the recovery room sometime after 6:30 P.M.

I had a horrible feeling when I looked around. None of the nurses was paying any attention to me. I had expected that they would rush over and tell me that I had a boy or a girl. I thought they were avoiding me because my baby had been still-born. In panic I screamed for a nurse and demanded that she call David.

What I didn't know was that David had not stayed around to

await the birth of our baby. He had gone off to the Wolkenbergs' apartment. But he had the good sense to leave their phone number, and the hospital reached him there.

As they wheeled me out of the recovery room, I opened my eyes and saw David standing over me with a big smile.

"It's a girl," he said. "She's beautiful . . . she looks just like you. . . ."

14

HOW E. J. KORVETTE
GOT DISCOUNTED

I spent three comfortable, happy days in the hospital. Seeing my little Cecilia at each feeding time was a joy I cannot describe. Although breast-feeding was the tradition in France, I was not anxious to follow that custom, for I did not believe in it. Aside from the bother it imposes on a mother, I felt it was an archaic way to feed a baby. My mother had breast-fed my sister, my brother, and me, and when she heard that I hadn't done the same for Cecilia, she hit the roof. My father had also been breast-fed—not by his mother, who was unable to, but by a wet nurse. Besides the fact that breast-feeding turns me off, my doctor had advised me not to do it, which was all the excuse I needed to justify my actions to my mother.

During my stay in the hospital I was swamped by a deluge of visitors. The Katzes, the Rosenfelds, the Kramers, the Wolkenbergs, Bernard Colson, and Robert Horn were among the friends and associates who came to see me and who brought gifts for the baby, who, I should not forget to mention, weighed a mere five pounds, four ounces. It was easy to see that Cecilia did not take after her father, who at the time weighed 195 pounds. I was just ninety-five pounds heavier than my daughter at birth!

One chilling memory remains from that otherwise pleasant stay in the hospital. Bob Horn came to visit on the second day and brought flowers. When the nurse unwrapped them and put them in the vase, an iceberg collided with my spine. They were chrysanthemums—the flowers that the French conventionally place on graves in tribute to the dead on All Saints Day. I said nothing to Bob about that, and I soon forgot the unintentional blunder by this American who knew nothing about French traditions. But two years later when I finally received my first letter from home, I learned that my father had died—on that very June 11, 1965, the day my baby was born.

I'll never forget when we brought Cecilia home. The apartment looked as though a cyclone had whirled through it. I expected to find the sink full of dirty, unwashed dishes, pots, and pans, and the bed unmade, because David was never meticulous about housekeeping. But the sight of the straw spread over the floor and furniture was too much. The straw had been used as packing in a large carton that had been delivered the day Cecilia was born. The box contained Cecilia's crib. When it was delivered, David and Bernard opened the carton and tried to put the crib together—without much success, I might add. In the process they scattered the packing straw helter-skelter over the apartment and never bothered to clean it up.

Rachel, a Jamaican girl we had retained as a nurse, and I put the crib together, and Cecilia had a place to sleep. Then came the monumental chore of cleaning up that mess.

I did not go to bed after that, nor follow my doctor's orders to stay off my feet and rest. Not when the proud papa was a gregarious, genial, hail-fellow-well-met monster. David wasted no time inviting friends over to the apartment from the moment we brought Cecilia home. He didn't just ask them over to see the baby, but he had them stay for lunch and dinner. And simple sandwiches wouldn't do for the visitors. Quiche Lorraine and salad had to be served for lunch. Then for dinner David would request we serve our guests *vol au vent fiancière* (a pastry shell filled with lobster) as an appetizer, stuffed roast veal for the main course, chocolate mousse for dessert, salad, cheese, and coffee.

Even with Rachel taking care of Cecilia's feedings and diaper changes and the help I had from Suzy, the Wolkenbergs' maid, I felt that no new mother had ever gone through what I had to endure. I was beyond weary. I was dragging myself around bleary-eyed and exhausted from catering to the interminable round of friends that David invited over. Fortunately, the merry-go-round ended after the first week, and I was able to enter a more normal existence as a mother and housekeeper.

Cecilia's birth was like a good-luck omen for us. From the moment we brought her home, David's career as an art dealer—in both legitimate and forged paintings—took a sharp upward spiral.

In no time at all, David had sold another four Chagalls and a Picasso to Mrs. Wolkenberg, who had found buyers for the paintings. These transactions swelled our bank balance by some seventeen thousand dollars—and that wasn't all. David was doing a brisk business at his gallery in the Empire State Building, selling other Chagalls, Picassos, Van Dongens, and Braques to dealers, galleries, and collectors.

With the capital David had amassed, he was able to branch out and buy legitimate works of art and sell these for substantial profit as well. But still he was operating on a relatively small scale.

The surge in sales did not go unnoticed by Lee Katz, who had an eye trained for businesses other than Kosher poultry. When he saw how well David was doing, Lee offered to join the Galerie Trianon as a partner. David was amenable to the suggestion, for he had a great deal of admiration and respect for Lee and felt he could get along well with him in a partnership. David, in fact, had no doubt that he would get along well with Lee, especially when the latter agreed to sink fifty thousand dollars into the gallery for a 50 percent cut of the business.

However, the partnership did not cross Lee's mind until David had been approached by none other than the top executives of E. J. Korvette, the nation's leading discount-department-store chain, which was planning to open a small art gallery in a corner of their huge Fifth Avenue store.

The business with E. J. Korvette all began when Bernard Colson heard that Korvette's was planning to open the gallery, mainly to compete with the nearby F. W. Woolworth's on Fifth Avenue, which had begun to sell expensive paintings. When Colson went to Korvette's, he sold the store a large number of graphics from the Galerie Maeght. During negotiations the store's officials asked Colson whether he could recommend any other dealers who could provide Korvette's with paintings.

"There is one dealer whom I recommend very highly," Colson said. "His name is David Stein."

A few days later, after an official from the store had gotten in touch with David and made an appointment, the doorbell of our apartment rang, and I admitted three visitors. One introduced himself as Eugene Ferkauf, the second as David Rothfeld, who was in charge of the department store's record-and-music sales division. I don't remember the name of the third man, but he was a Korvette's official, too.

I was extremely embarrassed to have these gentlemen in our apartment. I had no idea what kind of an operation Korvette's was. I was aware that it was a department-store chain, and in my naïve way I had made comparisons with Lord & Taylor and Saks Fifth Avenue. I felt very disconcerted that these distinguished gentlemen from such an elegant establishment would see our furnished flat with its "early motel" decor.

The visitors had hardly sat down and begun their discussions about buying paintings from David than they gazed at the collection of graphics hanging on our walls—Braques, Picassos, Bonnards, and Cassatts. Their admiration of the framed works was effusive. I couldn't help but admire their taste, for all of them were legitimate pieces. There wasn't a single David Stein forgery in the entire display.

Ferkauf asked David whether the paintings were for sale.

"Of course," David replied. "Do you have any one in mind?"

Ferkauf stood up, approached one of the Picassos, and said, "We'd like to buy this one."

Then Rothfeld rose from his chair, walked over to one of the Bonnards, and said, "This one, too."

Then Ferkauf pointed to a Braque that he liked and said he'd take that one as well. And that didn't end the buying spree. Taking turns, one after another, the three men from Korvette's singled out one piece after another until they had stripped our walls bare.

Fifteen paintings in all were bought that morning.

"Now, how much do you want for the whole lot?" Ferkauf asked David.

There was a stretch of silence as David stood nonplussed and speechless by the incredible quickness of the sale. It appeared as though it were up to David to break the silence. He did.

"Let's say ten thousand for everything," David suggested.

"Fine," Ferkauf said. "Bring them to our executive office, and we will draw up the check."

Before leaving, Ferkauf turned to David and asked, "By the way, have you any Chagall paintings?"

David thought hard.

"Not at the moment," he finally stammered, "but—but—I can get some for you in a few days."

"Fine, let me know when you can produce them, and I'll make an appointment for you to come down to the office and show them to me."

The word "produce" rattled me. Though I knew it was merely a figure of speech, I couldn't escape the thought of what must have been going through David's mind at the moment—he was going to take the drafting table out of the closet and begin mass-producing Chagalls.

David delivered the paintings off our walls to Korvette's the next day. He was ushered into Ferkauf's plush office on the Avenue of the Americas, and as David sat there chatting with him, a secretary brought in the ten-thousand-dollar check. Ferkauf handed it to David.

After examining the check, David looked at Ferkauf and asked, "How do I know it's good?"

Ferkauf gaped open-mouthed at David. Finally he blurted, "That's my signature on the check, isn't that good enough for you?"

"Well, I guess it's all right," David replied.

Later when he went back to his office in the Empire State Building and ran into Larry Kramer, the accountant, David related the episode to him.

"You really didn't say that to Ferkauf, did you?" Kramer asked incredulously.

"Yes, I did," David answered. "Why . . . what was wrong with that?"

"For Christ's sake, don't you know who Ferkauf is?" Larry demanded.

"No, who is he?" David asked, beginning to wonder.

"Why, why, he's been on the cover of *Time* magazine," Larry sputtered, almost unable to contain his exasperation. "And he also happens to be the president of Korvette's!" Larry added.

David took a deep breath and let it out. "Wheeeeeeeeew," he wheezed.

With that ten-thousand-dollar sale and with the fifty thousand that Lee Katz had put into the business as a partner, Galerie Trianon now had a healthy capitalization. David was finally in a position to wheel and deal in the grand manner. Or, as we say in French, *sur une grande échelle.* He could make some of the moves that weren't possible with his earlier restricted budget.

For some time now, David had had his eye on one of five huge Picasso oils on the subject of "The Rape of the Sabines" that was on display at the Picasso Arts Gallery in Manhattan. David had an idea the painting was going to command a big price, but he had no idea how big. He found out when he went to buy it—fifty thousand dollars.

And David bought it for fifty thousand dollars!

There wasn't any doubt in David's mind that he would have no trouble selling such an outstanding painting, for he knew full well that two of the oils in this series were already in museums. In his mind, too, was the thought that he might interest Korvette's in this Picasso.

It was with that objective in mind that he called Ferkauf and invited him to the Galerie Trianon. Ferkauf, who was soon to become chairman of Korvette's Board of Directors, arrived with Rothfeld. The visitors did not stay long, but again they showed an ability to come to quick decisions. They bought another fifteen paintings hanging in the gallery for another ten thousand dollars. But when David pulled out the prized Picasso, the executives balked.

"No," Ferkauf said, "we're not ready for anything that extravagant yet. We have allocated only a small corner of our store for paintings, and we certainly don't expect to sell works as expensive as this."

David was puzzled.

"What kind of an operation are you going to have?" he asked.

"It's hard to explain," Ferkauf said. "Why don't we drop into the store so you can see."

David agreed. He went with Ferkauf to the store, saw the space reserved for the art gallery, and shook his head.

"This is terrible," David said. "You just can't cram art into a small area like that. You must give it much more floor space."

That led to a long discussion about how an art gallery must be run. David poured forth his theories. It would be a great gimmick if Korvette's, the leading discount department store in the country, could apply its low-price policies in the sale of art. Not just inexpensive run-of-the-mill paintings and graphics, but bona fide Madison Avenue–type works.

David proceeded to explain to Ferkauf that the city's prestigious galleries work on large profit margins.

"For example," he said, " a gallery on Madison Avenue will buy a Chagall gouache for ten thousand dollars and sell it for sixteen thousand. Now, what you can do is buy that same Chagall and sell it for, say, twelve thousand. Doesn't a two-thousand-dollar profit appeal to you?"

Ferkauf smiled. The idea indeed appealed to him. Ferkauf took David to his office to carry on the discussion.

"What would you do if you were in my place?" Ferkauf wanted to know.

David suggested that Korvette's scuttle its plan to open its art gallery in its Fifth Avenue store, because limitations on space there drastically restricted the kind of operation he had in mind.

"Where do you have a store with space to spare?" David asked.

"We opened a very large store recently in Douglaston out in Queens," Ferkauf replied.

"I know the store," David said. "That's a very good location."

Korvette's followed David's suggestion. They never opened the art gallery on Fifth Avenue and, instead, built a wing onto their building in Douglaston. In October of that year they gave a gala opening that was attended by one of the largest assemblies of art dealers and collectors.

Among the "first-nighters" attending the opening was Sam Rosenfeld, whom we had met in Spain and who also dabbled in the buying and selling of art. Sam couldn't believe the bargain-basement prices that Korvette's had put on its paintings, and he proceeded to buy a whole raft of them.

"Boy," Sam said to David, "nobody can go wrong buying at these prices. I can sell these paintings for twice what I paid for them."

Long before Korvette's had opened its gallery in Douglaston, David fulfilled one of his ambitions—to unload that fifty-thousand-dollar Picasso. But not to Korvette's. The painting went to Lee Katz, whom David bought out as a partner two months after it all started. The business association ended after David decided he could do better without the restraints of a partner.

David had wanted to deliver the order of Chagalls to Ferkauf in the worst way, and he had only to sit down and paint a few forgeries. The temptation was great, but he simply wouldn't do that.

"No, Anne-Marie, I'm not doing it," David said. "I am not going to jeopardize the good thing I have going with Korvette's. We can make a fortune selling them authentic paintings, so why take chances?"

That is precisely what David did. The demand for paintings by Korvette's was so great that David spent most of his time touring the city's galleries for works that he sold exclusively to the department store. In fact, David made such a determined effort to satisfy Korvette's that he negotiated with the Galerie Maeght in Paris for one lonely but very legitimate Chagall which cost him ten thousand dollars. David sold it to Korvette's for twelve thousand, and the store, in turn, sold it to a collector for thirteen. This same Chagall would have commanded no less than eighteen thousand on Madison Avenue.

Incidentally, this particular Chagall was a drab watercolor depicting a rooster with a large blob of orange on its tail. I remember telling David, when I saw the painting, that he could have done much better.

But David was doing so much better by not painting Chagalls. The deal with Korvette's appeared to have all the promise of lasting forever and making us very rich. Orders kept pouring in, and David was worn to a frazzle chasing after paintings to keep Korvette's supplied.

And, of course, with so much money pouring in and the future looking so bright, it was only natural that David would want to move out of our furnished apartment in Rego Park and take up residence in a more prestigious locale. Lee Katz, who had found our flat in Queens, also had a hand in locating us a spacious apartment on the eighth floor of 525 Park Avenue.

We had many of the city's distinguished citizens living in our building. On our floor lived Mr. Rossuck, one of the top executives of the famed Wildenstein Gallery; on another floor lived Pauline Trigère, the haute couturière; and on still another floor resided Edward Gilbert, the financier, who lost his distinction when he got trapped in a Wall Street swindle, fled to South America, returned to surrender voluntarily, and ended up in the city's prison, the Tombs—at the very time that David was a guest there.

We spent twelve thousand dollars furnishing our new apartment, which isn't much by Park Avenue standards. But we bought furniture and furnishings judiciously. The apartment became not only our residence but David's art gallery as well. With a 525 Park Avenue address, who needed the Empire State Building?

Among our first visitors was Eugene Ferkauf, who seemed quite impressed with our elegant surroundings. He must have been, for he placed an order for eighty thousand dollars' worth of paintings.

Ferkauf, however, stiffened considerably in his future dealings with David. He became more of a bargainer, trying to shave the price of paintings that he was buying to the bare bone. I think Ferkauf had the mistaken notion that David was making a fortune from his sales to Korvette's, and he seemed determined to hold David's profits to a minimum.

David made one mistake in his dealings with Ferkauf. He should never have introduced him to Robert Horn, the owner of the Graphis Gallery. For Horn became friendly with Ferkauf and, in time, introduced him to Abe Lublin, the graphics publisher who had been buying David's forged Chagalls. Ferkauf's eye immediately went to the Chagall forgeries. And he bought them!

There was David doing his darndest to deal fairly and squarely with Korvette's, working on a relatively narrow margin of profit, sacrificing the opportunity to make a fortune by selling them his own fakes, and there was Eugene Ferkauf going behind David's back, so to speak, and buying the very forgeries that David had so zealously avoided unloading on Korvette's.

What an ironic way to get discounted!

15

MRS. EDWARD G. ROBINSON
IS DAVID'S ANGEL

From the day we moved into our six-hundred-dollar-a-month Park Avenue apartment, David became increasingly obsessed with luxuries and extravagances. Living in the midst of the jet set and involved with many of them in art deals, David was overcome with a compulsion to spend money. Traveling about town in taxis was no longer acceptable; David had to ride in a hired, chauffeur-driven limousine that cost forty dollars a day. And the $150 suits he had been wearing and regarded as the height of excellence in men's fashion were no longer for him; his new wardrobe was being reassembled with suits starting at $300. Nothing less would do. Our tab for dining out at La Caravelle, LePavillon, and many of the other fine French restaurants ran into thousands of dollars each month.

The big problem with David was that he was spending money before he had it. I warned him repeatedly that he was going over his head, but he wouldn't listen.

"I know what I'm doing," he would invariably say. "I don't want you to concern yourself with finances."

Time and again I reminded David about our red-inked checking-account balances. It was I, not he, who took the calls from the bank complaining that we were overdrawn. It was I who talked to creditors about our overdue bills.

What made the situation all the more disturbing around the latter part of October, 1965, was that Korvette's gallery had been stocked to its capacity with works of art, and whatever orders David was getting now were for replenishment of pieces being sold.

David's heavy concentration on selling paintings to Korvette's began to take its toll. He had neglected the galleries, dealers, and collectors with whom he had been doing business. All those introductions by Bernard Colson while helping David to launch his career had gone astray.

David had to start all over again. Although the people he had dealt with in the past still knew him, David had not sold them paintings for so long that many of his old customers felt neglected, and, after all, he wasn't the only art dealer in New York.

When things go bad, they have a way of getting worse.

One of the people we had met after moving into our Park Avenue apartment was Lynn Epstein, who came from a wealthy Chicago family. She was interested in art and occasionally bought paintings from David. In time, Miss Epstein became a free agent who bought and sold paintings, and today she has developed that activity into a gallery of her own in New York.

David's dealings with Miss Epstein led to what at the time threatened to be a near-cataclysmic encounter with the office of New York County District Attorney Frank Hogan. It happened this way:

Miss Epstein had introduced David to Richard Cohen, heir to the Goodman noodle fortune, who was looking to sell part of his father's collection of paintings and sculptures. Many of the sculpted works had been done by the noted German artist Käthe Kollwitz.

In the beginning Cohen brought the paintings to our gallery on the premise that David could find buyers for them. Most of the pieces were Grade B works of German expressionism, which is big in Munich, Stuttgart, Hamburg, and Frankfort but doesn't excite collectors or galleries in this country. David knew he'd find resistance in selling the works yet agreed to give it a try. But after the paintings had reposed in our gallery for a number of weeks without attracting a buyer, David returned the collection to Cohen.

Then Cohen came back with something else he wanted David to sell—a Käthe Kollwitz sculpture of the head of a woman. David was reluctant to take it.

"I don't deal in sculptures, I have no idea what the market value is, and I don't have any hope of finding a buyer," David said to Cohen.

But Cohen wouldn't take a refusal. "Keep it here in the gallery," he said. "Maybe someone will just walk in off the street and want to buy it."

Cohen seemed to think that selling paintings and sculptures was like merchandising noodles. Nevertheless, David took the bronze head and stuck it in a remote corner of the gallery. It reposed there unnoticed until Eva Lee, a gallery owner from Great Neck, Long Island, came in and took an interest in the head.

"How much do you want for this Kollwitz?" she asked.

"I have no idea what the market value is," David replied. "But if you're interested in it, you can take it on consignment and have it appraised somewhere. Then we'll both know what it's worth."

So Miss Lee took the bronze head and went to the Galerie Etienne in Manhattan. No sooner had she shown the sculpted work to the director than he disappeared into the back room. When he returned, he told her:

"I've called the district attorney's office. You are to wait here until one of their investigators comes. He wants to question you about that head."

"What's wrong with it?" Miss Lee asked in astonishment.

"This is a fake," the director said.

When the D.A.'s man arrived, he quizzed Miss Lee and learned that she had obtained the work from David. Actually, Miss Lee was an innocent victim of circumstances. She had done nothing wrong. If anything, she had been more conscientious than most dealers would have been in a similar situation. She went to an expert for an honest opinion on the worth of the sculpture—before trying to sell it. And she got the scare of her life for her integrity.

Miss Lee was not detained after her explanation as to where she had obtained the sculpture and that she was not selling it but merely trying to have it appraised. Although Miss Lee was permitted to leave, the bronze head was not. It was impounded by the D.A.'s investigator.

An hour later, Miss Lee returned to our gallery near tears to explain to David what had happened. "I had to tell him that I got it from you," Miss Lee said.

David was panic-stricken. He knew the D.A.'s office would be paying a visit to learn more about the sculpture.

David wasn't actually concerned about acquitting himself in the rhubarb over the bronze head. He could prove easily enough that it had been left at Trianon on consignment from Richard Cohen, and any further explanations would have to come from him. But what terrified David was what would happen to us once the D.A.'s people began probing our backgrounds, which we felt certain they would do. How would we explain our illegal arrival in the United States?

We were so accustomed to the French police system which, as we knew it then, was very thoroughgoing and harsh. We had very little awareness at that time of the methods the police in the United States employed. We could only think of what the French authorities would do in similar circumstances—hours and hours of questioning, deep probing of our backgrounds even to the point of demanding to know our lineal ancestry.

We were pleasantly surprised—and greatly relieved—to find that authorities in the United States don't go to such extremes.

Our fears and apprehensions were quickly put to rest when Assistant District Attorney Joseph Stone, now a Criminal Court judge, dropped into our gallery with Detective Nicholas J. Barrett. They asked a few simple questions: Did we know the sculpture was a fake? Where did we get it? Hardly anything more than that.

David explained the circumstances that led to his having the head, and that quickly satisfied the D.A.'s men, who then took off.

I don't know what course the investigation took after that, but I'm reasonably confident the prosecutor's probers had some questions to ask Cohen. However, neither Cohen nor his father got into any difficulty.

Just as Richard Cohen was going out of our life, Louis D. Cohen, a multimillionaire real-estate operator from Great Neck and Palm Beach, came in. Louis Cohen had become interested in art and was trying to start a collection. Eugene Ferkauf, the merchandising mogul-turned-art-connoisseur, was a good friend of Cohen's, and sent him to our gallery to look around.

But Cohen couldn't make up his mind about any of the hundreds of works hanging in our gallery. He visited Trianon again and again without buying. Finally he became interested in a Dufy watercolor and gouache titled "The Concert." But he didn't inform David that he had decided to buy it until he had gone off to Palm Beach for the winter. Then one day Cohen phoned New York and told David, "My chauffeur will be in to pick up that Dufy."

The conversation didn't end there. Cohen had some thoughts he wanted to share with David.

"Why don't you bring some of your paintings down here?" he suggested. "I may want to buy something else. But even if I don't, I can introduce you to a lot of wealthy people who will probably be very interested in your collection."

The invitation appealed to David. Though we had nearly $200,000 worth of paintings hanging in our gallery, the balance in our checking account was an enemic $700. Business was still not going well. David was selling a painting here and a painting there, but whatever profits he made were being used either to purchase other art works or for our high style of living. The thought of busting into Palm Beach's millionaire's row and its claque of high-society colonists made David drool.

In mid-January David kissed me *au revoir* as he left me to mind the store and flew to the sun-kissed state. He took along a small collection of original paintings. What weighed down his luggage more than anything was the supply of "aged" drawing paper and pastels, watercolors, and other art supplies. David had larceny in his heart.

David checked into a sixty-dollar-a-day room in the plush Colony Hotel. Such a high overhead normally wouldn't matter while David was producing forgeries, because the profits from the sale of the fakes more than adequately covered all expenses. But David's initial dealings in Palm Beach didn't give him that much of a margin. In fact, he lost money. That was because he was dealing with Louis Cohen, an exercise in total frustration for David, who could never get the price he asked for from this wily million-aire. Cohen hacked and hewed at every one of David's quota-tions.

David sold Cohen three more paintings besides the Dufy that the chauffeur picked up in New York. These were a Picasso oil, a Picasso gouache, a di Chirico oil, all legitimate works, and an assortment of fakes that David painted in his hotel room espe-cially for Cohen as a hedge against the beating he knew he was going to take on the real works.

But even with the forgeries David unloaded on Cohen it was a losing proposition. Cohen had paid David approximately $20,000 for the whole package. When we finally held an accounting of the transaction, we found that we had lost money. The originals that David had sold to Cohen had cost us $22,000! You can imag-ine how much deeper in the red David would have gone had he not palmed off the forged Picassos and other fakes on Cohen.

David had to turn elsewhere in Palm Beach to recoup.

With his handsome good looks, charisma, charm, warm per-sonality, and French accent, David cut quite a swath with the ladies at the Colony, many of them lonely because their hus-bands were busy watching the ticker tape on Wall Street up yonder in New York. And when they saw David in his unat-tached state, they flocked to him.

One of the ladies who took a more than casual interest in David was Gladys Lloyd Robinson, whose former husband, Ed-ward G. Robinson, needs no introduction. Gladys and Edward were divorced by then, but during the long years of their mar-riage Mrs. Robinson and her husband had amassed an amazing collection of paintings which, conservatively estimated, had a net worth of more than five million dollars. At the time of their di-vorce, Robinson and his wife divided their art collection in half. Mrs. Robinson then sold a large part of her share of the paintings for something like two million to Stavros Niarchos, the Greek shipping magnate. However, Mrs. Robinson remained involved with the art world, for she was painting, too.

When she met David, Mrs. Robinson found a common interest which quickly developed into a warm friendship. David be-came Mrs. Robinson's escort. He took her to parties, and she introduced him to scores of people. Among them were Alfred

Cass, a former ambassador; Mrs. Frances Spingold, wife of Nathan B. Spingold, of Columbia Pictures; George Schrafft, owner of the Schrafft restaurant chain; Russian Prince Nikky Toumanoff; Marjorie Meriweather Post, the cereal heiress; Charles Dubois, of Dubois Chemical; and Jim Kimberly, of Kimberly-Clark Corporation.

As David was meeting all these beautiful people, the wheels in his mind were turning. What an opportunity to zap them, David told himself. All that wealth! What paintings he could sell them!

In addition, Mrs. Robinson served as the catalyst to launch David's grand design. It happened at the Red Cross Ball in late January. Mrs. Robinson had donated a painting that was to be auctioned at the affair. When the auctioneer asked for bids, David deliberately leaped right into the thick of it. He finally got the painting when his two-thousand-dollar bid couldn't be topped.

Next day, the Palm Beach newspapers published David's picture on page one with the story of his purchase of Mrs. Robinson's painting. David Stein was a hero, for he had outbid some of the biggest pocketbooks in the country. The publicity was a press agent's dream, and that was all the push David needed.

He decided to open an art gallery in Palm Beach.

16

THE F.B.I. COMES
TO DAVID'S RESCUE

When David called me in New York and told me he had decided to open a branch of the Galerie Trianon in Palm Beach, I thought he was *non compos mentis*. Or *fou*, as we say in French.

"What are you going to use for money?" I asked.

"Don't worry, *chérie*," he consoled me. "I have a very fat pigeon who is buying my paintings and will buy many more."

He was referring to Louis D. Cohen, or L.D., as David called him. Cohen had brought David down to Palm Beach and now had talked him into the idea of opening a gallery. Cohen had even taken David to the bank and showed him thirty thousand dollars that was stashed in a safe-deposit box.

"He told me all that money I saw there could be mine if I give him a decent break on paintings," David said to me. "So you see, the money is there to open the gallery in Palm Beach."

David wanted me to pack our belongings and come down— with Cecilia, of course. I couldn't believe the glowing forecast of instant riches that David suggested were ours in that Florida playpen of millionaires. Nevertheless, I followed David's instructions. At least I'd see for myself what it was like down there, and if I didn't like what I saw, I could always return home. After all, I loved what we had in New York. Our apartment on Park Avenue was the first really decent home I'd had since I left Avignon.

It had the permanence that none of the places where David and I had stayed had ever afforded. My decision to join David was also influenced by an awareness that we wouldn't be in Palm Beach too long, for the winter season had only two short months to run. Once spring came, David would have to close the gallery just as most of the other shop owners did.

David was waiting for Cecilia and me when we landed at the West Palm Beach Airport, and we were driven to the Colony in a Silver Cloud Rolls Royce with a chauffeur behind the wheel.

"I am not paying him much," David said to me about the chauffeur. "Only a hundred fifty a week."

It seemed like a bargain compared with New York, where it cost us forty dollars a day for a hired car and its liveried driver.

"That is because I bought the car," David added, which was a shock to me. "You know, *chérie,* you are a nobody down here if you don't drive a Rolls."

We stopped at the Colony only long enough for me to freshen up and to learn some additional details about David's plan to expand Trianon's operations in Palm Beach. He had already found the store, hired a designer and architect, and renovations had begun. He took me to see the new Galerie Trianon.

If I tell you I was stunned when I saw the empty store, I would be understating. It was on fashionable Worth Avenue, where all the most prestigious shops were situated. What really impressed me was the next-door tenant—Van Cleef & Arpels. The premises David had rented had been occupied before by the Galerie Félix Vercel, which had closed at the end of the 1964–65 winter season and did not reopen for 1965–66.

I had serious apprehensions about the enterprise, but I also had confidence in David, and I didn't want to be an anchor around his neck or sound like a nagging wife. I told myself that if anyone could sell paintings in Palm Beach, David could. He deserved a chance to test his mettle in that environment.

What I objected to most of all was that sixty-dollar-a-day tab at the Colony. David agreed it was high, so he found an apartment on Chilean Avenue. It was furnished in the most luxurious style imaginable. And it should have been, for the rent was $750 a month. But that was still a lot less than the $1,800 it was costing at the hotel.

Not many days after our arrival in Palm Beach, the Galerie Trianon was ready to open its doors. David went to great lengths to make the *vernissage* something to remember. The reception David had made for himself in Palm Beach circles by buying Mrs. Robinson's painting went a long way in winning friends among the Social Registerites. And when he sent out invitations to the privileged classes—he culled the Social Register for names and addresses—they turned out in droves to the opening.

It was an opening to remember. How can I forget it—$700 worth of liquor for the guests, who drank us dry. Later, we gave a dinner party at the Colony for fifteen special people who had been helpful to David in Palm Beach. Among them were Alice Bogan and the William Findlays, Senior and Junior.

The Findlays were in our crowd because David had made arrangements with them to provide our gallery with paintings from their distinguished gallery in Chicago. David wasn't really the reason why the William Findlays had agreed to install a large collection of their best paintings in the Trianon. They had a far more compelling reason.

For years there had been a bitter rivalry with the elder William Findlay's brother, Wally, who owned the famed Wally Findlay Gallery just down the street from our Palm Beach gallery. To complete the picture, a third Findlay brother, David, owned the renowned David Findlay Gallery on East Fifty-seventh Street in New York. Wally had made a career of competing with his two brothers. He opened galleries in New York and Chicago.

Now, through their association with David and Trianon, the William Findlays decided to make things warm for Wally in Palm Beach. To that end, they shipped more than $200,000 worth of paintings from New York via air freight. But the works of art never reached our gallery for the opening.

The shipment, containing canvases by Renoir, Pissarro, Matisse, Chagall, Valadon, and Dufy, was mistakenly delivered to the Wally Findlay Gallery, although the shipping labels clearly listed the addressee as William Findlay, care of Galerie Trianon.

When the paintings failed to reach us in time for the opening and did not arrive the following day, David called the Railway Express Agency and queried them about the shipment. R.E.A., which for decades had been losing deliveries shipped on the nation's railroads, had now branched out into air freight with the same bad habits. R.E.A. checked its records and found that the driver had delivered the paintings to Wally Findlay's gallery in error. A promise was given that the shipment would be retrieved from Wally's place at once and delivered to us.

When the R.E.A. man went to Findlay's, however, no one seemed to know anything about the shipment from New York. Although the driver had a receipt signed by the Findlay Gallery's girl friday, she just couldn't remember what happened to the paintings, and Wally was nowhere to be found. Even if she could locate the paintings, the girl told the driver, she could never release them unless Wally was there.

The William Findlays didn't take kindly to the situation, since it involved more than $200,000 worth of art work. Worse, it involved their brother Wally. They stopped shadowboxing and went straight to the authorities. In a matter of hours the investigation took on the magnitude of an all-out search by the Palm Beach police, insurance-company detectives, and even the Federal Bureau of Investigation, since this was an interstate shipment.

It took the better part of the next day to trace the missing canvasses. Eventually, they were ferreted out by the F.B.I. from a second-floor storage room in Wally Findlay's gallery, a very strange place to store a shipment of valuable works of art unless you are trying to "lose" them.

The F.B.I. agents delivered the masterpieces to David, who thanked them in his best illegal-alien English. Then David proceeded to hang the works in the gallery. Now we thought we were really in business. But even with the William Findlay exhibit and all the other legitimate works that David had bought and put on display in the gallery, business was slow.

In the remaining two months of the winter season we did a modest business at best, but it was not nearly enough to pay for the expenses we were incurring—rent for the gallery, rent for our apartment in Palm Beach, rent for our gallery-apartment on Park Avenue, not to forget David's extravagant tastes. Our restaurant and bar tabs alone in Palm Beach were more than five hundred dollars a week.

Even David was beginning to agree that we weren't going to get out of Palm Beach without severe losses. So to cut that deficit to a bare minimum, he decided that he had to revert to painting and selling his forgeries.

One of his first targets was Charles Dubois, the chemical tycoon, for whom David painted two Chagall gouaches, one featuring a rooster, the other a pair of lovers. But before David embarked on that escapade, he turned to me and said, "*Chérie*, will you brew some strong tea. . . ."

When I had added ten years to the life of the paper, David broke out his paints, and it was just like old times. Dubois bought the pair of Chagalls for $10,000, a deal that netted us a $9,917.96 profit. Where did the $82.04 go? Let me break it down because I haven't yet shown you how much it costs to produce a fake. Here is the capital required for one David Stein Chagall:

Tea, 2¢; paper, $3.00; colors, $8.00; framing, $30.00 (we always gave a good frame).

So with an investment of $41.02—not counting David's time at the drawing board, which usually amounted to an hour or two per painting—he could realize a net yield on a $5,000 sale of $4,958.98.

David made nowhere near that on the two Chagalls he had sold to L. D. Cohen earlier. Though the paintings were every bit as well done as the ones he sold Dubois, Cohen refused to pay more than $4,000 for the two of them. On that particular transaction David could have netted a respectable $3,917.96 profit had not Cohen complicated the deal. He insisted that David sell him a Valtat oil as well, which was an original that David had wanted to sell for $2,000, exactly what it had cost him. But Cohen worked on David and got it for $1,400.

What really inspired David to return to forgery, although the desperate need to stave off losses was a prime consideration, was an exhibit at another of the city's galleries, the Phipps, which had just received an important shipment of paintings in Palm Beach from the famed Hirschl and Adler Gallery in New York. David and I received invitations to view the exhibit.

As we were strolling through the gallery with the crowd of millionaires and society folk, David and I almost choked on our champagne when we spotted a Chagall hanging in a prominent place on one of the walls. There was something familiar about that watercolor-and-gouache painting featuring a donkey, flying ballerina, and fiddler floating in the sky.

"Does that Chagall remind you of something?" I heard David whispering in my ear.

"It does, it does," I stammered but not quite certain of just what memory the painting held for David. I knew I had seen it before, because I recognized it as one of David's fakes. But I couldn't remember where David had sold it.

"Which one is it?" I asked David almost under my breath, for we were accompanied on our tour of the Phipps Gallery by Mr. and Mrs. Sam Dingman, of Canada.

It was one of the two paintings that Bryan, the pickpocket, had unlimbered on the O'Hanna Gallery in London for three thousand pounds! Seeing the Chagall hanging in the Phipps Gallery certainly was inspiring, but what was even more stimulating was the price tag. Phipps was selling this fake for eleven thousand dollars!

David's most memorable—and most profitable—sale in Palm Beach was that Picasso gouache, the atelier, which David had painted in twelve hours in our Rego Park apartment and which he refused to sell to Sears, Roebuck for fourteen thousand dollars because he had insisted on eighteen thousand.

It was almost a year later now, and David still had the Picasso—hanging in the window of the Galerie Trianon in Palm Beach. It had been hanging there since opening day. There'd been many inquiries about the painting, but no one was willing to shell out the eighteen thousand that David was still asking.

Then along came Colonel George Garbisch, who was the husband of one of the Chrysler daughters, an heiress of the automobile fortune.

"How much is that Picasso?" asked Garbisch.

"I am asking eighteen thousand for it," David said.

The colonel shook his head. "Too much."

"What is your price?" David wanted to know.

"I'll give you fourteen thousand," the colonel offered.

"It's yours, Colonel," David said.

Later David told me:

"I had to sell it to Garbisch for fourteen thousand. He shook me up when he mentioned that figure. After all, Sears offered me fourteen thousand. Maybe that's all it's worth. . . ."

Toward the end of February, it was the beginning of the end of the winter vacation season in Palm Beach and the beginning of the end for the Galerie Trianon. The socialites and millionaires were heading north to spend a brief while at their "permanent" residences before flying off to summer vacation spas. Our days in Palm Beach were numbered.

David decided to return to New York and pay attention to the Trianon there. I had left the gallery in charge of a competent manager who had made some important sales of legitimate paintings, but the transactions were nothing to rave about. David was desperate to generate new business. Also, he had to prepare the gallery for a benefit exhibition that had been arranged months before for Brandeis University.

David left me and Cecilia in Palm Beach. I was to close the gallery and wind up our business affairs, then come home.

David's return to New York was marked by a new turn of direction. He plunged into preparations for the Brandeis show, which was aimed at raising funds through the sale of art for the university. Out of these sales, Trianon was to realize some 70 percent of the proceeds, the university 30 percent.

But opening day, which is the most important one in the duration of any art exhibit, turned into a dismal failure. It had rained all day, heavily. The downpour kept the crowd to a couple of dozen prospective buyers, and they bought a mere five hundred dollars' worth of paintings, strictly poverty-row business.

David went back to the drawing board to create forgeries, which, when you look at it soberly, had been his only means of making big money. He plunged into a mass-production of Chagalls. That's all the buying public wanted. David painted Chagalls, Chagalls, and more Chagalls. He painted every version—gouaches, pastels, watercolors, and mixed media. The subjects touched upon every character and scene Chagall had ever created—the clowns, the lovers, the donkeys, the roosters, the ballerinas, and the Russian villages. David sold these paintings for prices ranging from a minimum $2,500 to a very respectable $9,000, and he was "back in business."

Meanwhile, I was going out of my mind in Palm Beach. The

winter season had ended. Everybody was gone, the Colony was closed, the shops along Worth Avenue were shuttered, and there I was watching TV all day long. I saw every *77 Sunset Strip* episode ever shown, not to mention the stupid soap operas and movie reruns.

My emancipation from Palm Beach came just before Mother's Day of 1966. I received a call from David.

"Now that you have wound up our affairs down there, what are you waiting for?" he said. "Come home."

No one ever left Palm Beach in greater haste than I. When we arrived in New York, Cecilia and I were picked up in our chauffeur-driven limousine and taken not to our apartment but to the Beekman Hotel where David was staying.

I could never understand it. David had a compulsion to hole up at expensive hotels whenever I was separated from him for any period of time. The summer before when we were still living in Rego Park, I had gone off to Southampton for a few days' respite, and David went off to stay at the St. Regis Hotel.

Our stay at the Beekman lasted just over the weekend. On Monday we went back to 525 Park Avenue. I'm happy that we went back on the day following Mother's Day, for I had a very important announcement for David. I was pregnant again.

17

DAVID BECOMES
A DRUG ADDICT

As a Frenchman, David always subscribed to the pleasure of gourmet dishes. He could never adapt to the custom of eat-and-run nourishment that seems to sustain such a large segment of American society.

When it was time for lunch or dinner, David had to have a sit-down meal. He was not a glutton, yet he ate with a lusty appetite. The consequences began to show at this juncture of his life as he passed his thirty-first birthday. My five-foot, seven-inch David was tipping the scales at two hundred pounds. He was obviously overweight, and to make matters worse, the doctor who examined him found that David had an ulcer.

The doctor put David on a strict diet. He was to eat broiled lean meat and fish, boiled fresh vegetables, and fresh fruit. Fats, starches, and sweets were out. David didn't mind the limitations and restrictions imposed on his eating style, but what really drove him up the wall was the medical order not to drink alcohol. That was a terrible imposition on a man like David, who loved red wines, Scotch, and brandy with a passion.

Despite all the prohibitions against eating and drinking, David managed to survive. His blood pressure had risen to dangerous levels, and the threat of a heart attack was increasing with each pound he added to his corpulent contours. But his diet, or rather the medication, had a devastating side effect. At first, the doctor prescribed amphetamine pills, which David took at home. Then the doctor decided to increase the dosage and began to give David injections of a drug combined with B-12. At the outset the one-a-day shots seemed to give David the strength to keep him propped against the drawing board for long hours turning out forgeries.

This was David's most productive period as a faker of the masters, or rather *the* master. The demand for Chagalls now exceeded anything we'd ever experienced. Suddenly, all New York, indeed the entire country, was bidding for them. Chagall had recently completed the celebrated stained-glass windows for the synagogue of the Hadassah Medical Center in Jerusalem, was putting the finishing touches to the ceiling of the Paris Opera, and was soon to come to New York to hang his mural at the new Metropolitan Opera House in Lincoln Center.

David could have become a millionaire many times over if he had kept up with the demand. He could knock off a Chagall by now in an hour or less and sell it for several thousand dollars. But as I have stressed so many times before, in the ever-perilous quicksands of art forgery one must not become a glutton and flood the market with fakes. Moderation is the key to success. The same rule applies to counterfeiters of ten- and twenty-dollar bills.

Art forgery, however, is an even more precise science, for it requires far greater discrimination while marketing fakes. The art world is a relatively small business, and as Abe Lublin put it, "If someone sneezes in New York, somebody says gesundheit in Los Angeles." Once a Chagall is sold, especially to a gallery or a dealer, word gets around quickly that the work is on the market. Other galleries or dealers hungry for Chagalls inquire where the work was bought. Then they proceed to seek their own Chagalls from that source. If a forger does not tread cautiously and instead keeps up with the demand, very soon the buyers that he has attracted will begin to get suspicious and ask how it is possible for him to obtain all those Chagalls. Such a faker will inevitably become the richest man—in jail.

There is another trap that an art forger must be wary of—the Internal Revenue Service. You have no idea how many times I warned David. Although David saved his bills of sales, he established no proof of acquisition for the paintings he forged.

During this period David sold four more Chagalls to Abe Lublin. It was a day early in June. David had been on his diet for some three weeks by then, and he was getting daily drug injections at the doctor's office, just a short walking distance from our Park Avenue apartment.

"*Chérie*," David said as he walked in just before dinner, "what good news do you think I have brought from Abe?"

"He wants us for a weekend at his country home," I smiled. "And his mother-in-law is going to cook dinner for us. . . ."

I simply loved her cooking. After all, she was French.

"Better than that," David came back. "Abe is going to give me ten thousand dollars tomorrow morning."

"A loan?" I asked.

"No. He is buying four Chagalls from me," David said.

"But you don't have any Chagalls here," I said without thinking. Then I began to laugh as order returned to my mind. If David didn't have four Chagalls when he got up the next morning, it would be a sure bet that he'd have four Chagalls by noon.

As it turned out, David arose at 6 A.M., had a light diet breakfast that the doctor commanded him to eat, and then went to his drawing board. He painted the last brush stroke two hours before the deadline. Yes, David painted four Chagalls in a little more than three hours!

Lublin loved each of the paintings. Not only did he pay David the ten thousand dollars that had been in David's mind from the moment Lublin had ordered the Chagalls the previous afternoon, but our benefactor then brought David and me to his country home for the weekend and to a delightful French meal prepared by his wonderful mother-in-law, who I very regretfully must report has since passed away.

In the weeks that followed, David produced many more fakes, all Chagalls, which he sold to John Marqusee, a wealthy collector and friend of Lublin, Frank Morini, an art dealer, and Edwin Bachman, also an art dealer and through whom David met Fernand Legros, the art dealer from Paris who was immortalized in Clifford Irving's book *Fake!*

It was in Bachman's apartment that David was shown with

great pride a valued work by one of the foremost post-Impressionist masters, Gauguin.

"What do you think of this masterpiece?" asked Bachman, for whom the business of dealing in paintings had passed from a hobby to a full-time occupation after he had given up being concert master for Toscanini.

Without much more than a glance at the painting, David turned to Bachman and said, "It's a fake."

Bachman was staggered. He didn't want to believe it.

"That cannot be," he protested. "I got that painting from Legros—and you know his reputation."

"That's what I mean," David returned with a smile.

Then switching to business, David said to Bachman, "I have something very special to offer you . . . are you interested?"

"If you say Chagall, I am interested," Bachman said.

That evening, David ripped off two more Chagalls but in nowhere near the time of his previous efforts. It had taken him five hours to paint this pair of fakes. As I watched David at the drawing board discarding one false start after another, I couldn't help but wonder what was wrong with him. Then I realized what had been happening.

His condition had been building up slowly. At first it was almost imperceptible, but yet I was aware even then that something wasn't right with David. He was irritable and short-tempered. When the condition became aggravated, I became alarmed. He would fly off the handle at the slightest provocation. He abused good friends, insulted business associates, and threw violent fits of rage in the house.

I finally discovered what was causing David's distressing display of temper—those drug injections. By now they weren't being administered at the rate of one a day—but four and five a day. And the diet had gone out the window. David was drinking at a furious pace. Not really more than he'd been drinking before he went on the diet, but the amount of alcohol he was taking, combined with the drug in such large doses, was working devastation on David.

As I look back now, I blame myself for not having taken a more aggressive interest in David's condition. I knew what was happening, but I was not assertive enough to stop it. If I had to do it over, I would have the district attorney arrest the doctor for administering a drug in excessively dangerous dosages. When I tried to convince David that he was taking too many injections, he would tell me to shut up and to mind my own business.

"Don't you think the doctor knows what he is doing?" he would scream at me.

Yes, I believe the doctor knew what he was doing. At $10 a shot, he was making $50 a day off David, and if you consider that this went on every day, that amounted to $350 a week.

David was no different from the city's other drug addicts who bought their "stuff" on street corners and mainlined it in back alleys. Except that what David was doing was legal, because it was happening in a doctor's office on Park Avenue.

I would like to tell you that David kicked his drug habit, but I cannot say it. The doctor didn't let him. It was too profitable for him. Although David gave up his habit during our short stay in Palm Beach, he went back on the amphetamines after we came back to New York and remained a drug addict down to the very end.

18

OUR SUMMER
OF DISCONTENT

Despite David's hair-trigger temper, his refusal to listen to reason, and his continued spree on drugs, he was turning out Chagalls at a phenomenal pace. He was making money, as the expression goes, hand over fist, but it was going faster than he was making it.

Moreover, David had by now become obsessed with the belief that he was invincible. The drug injections had him flying high, believing he could accomplish anything, not only in forging the works of the masters but in any other endeavor. But David stuck to his drawing board painting Chagalls at a clip that may have even exceeded Chagall himself.

David was beginning to hallucinate.

"Look at what I have accomplished in one year," he would say to me. "I have a big art gallery on Park Avenue, I am riding in my own Rolls Royce with my own chauffeur, I have sold Korvette's a half-million dollars' worth of paintings, I took over Palm Beach society, and I have fooled some of the world's greatest art experts with my forgeries."

But our bank account did not reflect these great accomplishments. I was getting calls almost every day from the manager of the Chemical Bank that we were overdrawn.

Why were we overdrawn? Consider these expenses for the month of June, 1966:

Doctor's bill for David's drug injections	$1,400.00
Maid service	360.00
Rent	600.00
Telephone	1,500.00
Restaurants	800.00
Chauffeur (also doubling now as man-servant for David at increased salary)	800.00
Food and liquor at the apartment	700.00
Electricity and gas	100.00

Our expenses were $6,260 a month—without even including clothes, cleaning bills, newspapers, magazines, and sundry other items.

So, while David was making big money selling his fakes during June, July, and August of 1966, the expenses we were incurring—and the outstanding debts that David had entered into in the months before—were draining every cent of income he was making. The whole problem was that David was spending the money even before he was making it—in fact, long before he was making it.

His output of Chagalls reached a high-water mark in August. He sold eighteen of the master's fakes for an average of $3,500 each, or a total of $63,000. And, would you believe it, we were deeper in debt than ever before!

During this time I had gone through my first six months of pregnancy without any of the difficulties I had encountered while I was carrying Cecilia. Not one hemorrhage in this period. The doctor assured me that I was home free with my second birth. David and I were both hoping the baby was a boy, but neither of us really cared. Cecilia was such a beautiful baby that neither of us would have minded, really, if I had given birth to another girl.

Meanwhile, it wasn't a "lost weekend." It was a lost summer. We stayed in New York. We could no longer afford the luxury of Southampton or any other seaside resort. David was painting and selling Chagalls and getting deeper into debt. I was really worried.

David was one of the world's most loquacious speakers on the phone. He talked not for minutes, but for hours, to friends and acquaintances in Europe, which is why our phone bill was fifteen hundred a month.

Friends and acquaintances weren't the only ones David talked to. A time came in August when David suddenly turned to me and said, "Why the hell don't I call my mother?"

I had never been too impressed by David's relationship with his mother. I had never met the woman, and although David always spoke kindly of her, I had the distinct notion that she was basically a very selfish woman. From what David had said about her, she seemed not only parsimonious but egocentric. According to David, she constantly imposed her will on him and made him give in to her every wish and command.

The first twenty-nine years of David's life were influenced to a large extent by his mother. Part of that sway was generated by Leonne Haddad's loneliness—and helplessness—that followed the death of her second husband, Henry, David's father.

Until then it had been a close-knit happy family with David's two half-brothers, François and Robert, and half-sister, Madeleine. David, who was born in Colombes, outside Paris, spent almost all of his life in the French capital. They lived in a fashionable apartment house at 6 Avenue Dode de la Brunerie, not far from the famed Auteuil Racetrack.

The family enjoyed a comfortable life, for David's father was a good provider who treated his stepsons with the same care and compassion that he gave his own boy. But deep down his father had special affection and love for David, not only because he was his own flesh and blood but, as David has often said, "because he fathered me so late in life."

David's father, a medical doctor who had spent many years at the Pasteur Institute, opened his own hospital in Colombes, an institution that he continued to operate until his death. The income was good and enabled him not only to move his family into their chic living quarters in Paris but also to provide them with many luxuries that they might not have enjoyed if he had continued to toil unrewardingly as most researchers do at the Pasteur Institute.

The most tragic memory of childhood that David retained was the disappearance—and apparent death—of his half-brother François, who was seized on the Spanish border by the Nazis while trying to reach England and join De Gaulle's forces. David's greatest respect for his mother was rooted in his admiration of her relentless search after the war to learn what had happened to François.

David's father died in 1950 at the age of sixty when David was fifteen years old. It was a most shattering experience for David, who loved his father with an ardor I cannot describe. He saw his papa die before his very eyes of a massive heart attack. David was left with many unhappy memories, and often he would talk about his childhood with great detail.

David was born on January 25, 1935—exactly 179 years after Mozart. To honor the birthday of this great man and his son, David's father decided not to buy the diamond brooch he was planning to give his wife, but to buy a grand piano for his new son instead. And on David's fifth birthday, his father sat him down before that piano.

David's father spent what rare moments of relaxation he knew listening to operatic arias. He particularly liked Italian tenors. David's fondest recollection of those moments was when his father would signal him to rewind the phonograph. David would walk up to the machine and turn the handle, his eyes riveted on the little dog trademark of "His Master's Voice," his ears filled with the lilting voices of Enrico Caruso and Tito Schipa.

Although David hadn't yet learned to read music at that early age, he was soon able to play by ear.

"I always played the first few measures of everything—*La Bohème, Carmen*, and *Madame Butterfly*," David told me.

His father was so astonished when David could play so well that he immediately engaged a piano teacher for him. In a few months little David was playing Mozart's *Marche Turque*.

"I can still hear the metronome as it beat out the measure every afternoon at four o'clock, the hour of my lesson," I remember David telling me one night.

Besides the love he held for music, David's father also was

interested in art and collected paintings. David remembers those paintings that his father acquired and hung up on the walls of their apartment—works by Isabey, Tiepolo, Courbet, and even a number of studies in charcoal that his father himself had done in his youth. But David was most impressed with Guido Reni's "Saint Sebastian" which hung above the gray marble mantel of the fireplace, opposite the piano.

"That painting had me hypnotized," David would tell me. "Those moments of giddiness when I desperately tried to uncover and comprehend the secrets behind its creation are still fresh in my mind. Balancing myself on the armrest of a chair, I would draw myself up so close to the painting that I could no longer distinguish the shapes."

That Saint Sebastian belonged to the world of David's childhood. He felt the same affinity with Sebastian as most other little boys his age had felt with Mickey Mouse. But neither the saint nor his creator would ever know that they were the cause of David's first major crisis of his childhood.

One day while he was practicing scales on the piano, his stepbrother Robert, who was five years older than David, walked into the room in his usual guise of fierce warrior, armed with his carbine and rubber arrows.

"He aimed at me," I remember David saying, "then pointed his gun at that which he knew to be the object of my love. With all the cruelty and sadism that a boy of ten can possibly contain, he let fly at my Saint Sebastian, which was already riddled with holes. . . ."

David's voice broke, I can recall, as he spoke about that sad childhood experience.

"Then I could only weep," David went on. "Later, I knew Robert had committed a sacrilege."

David has always felt that Sundays are sad. He felt they were more so during his childhood because of his terror of German soldiers who were occupying France. What made it all the worse for his father and the other members of the family was that they had to wear the yellow star of David sewn on their outer garments.

"In an effort to escape that menacing reality," David told me, "my father accustomed me to the serenity of museums, where the only sound we heard was that of our wooden-soled shoes resounding in the vast rooms."

Sunday was always David's day at the museum, and every Sunday his father acquainted his son with Rembrandt, Corot, Van Dyck, Géricault, Delacroix, and the other masters. Sometimes his father even took David to the Louvre, at other times to Le Jeu de Paume, the Orangerie, or the Luxembourg Museum.

"When we returned home," David told me, "I would urge my papa to show me reproductions in his books of the works I had seen that afternoon."

Although David liked to sketch and experiment with color, and apart from Latin, geography, and mathematics, which he didn't understand at all, it was music above all that took up most of his time as an adolescent and young teen-ager. His dream was to become a concert pianist.

He had begun to fulfill that dream at the Paris Conservatory under Jacques Thibaud and Marguerite LeLong, who gave up a brilliant career on the concert stage to devote herself to teaching others. At the end of the year, David had been awarded first place in the conservatory's competition, and Madame LeLong said to him, "You have the hands of a great pianist."

Then in his second year his father died. Visits to museums, hours of reading in the library, and even his studies at the conservatory and dreams of becoming a pianist came to an end.

On that day, David had returned home as usual from classes. He'll never forget the day or the hour—a Monday, six o'clock in the evening. His last class was French.

"My father had taken ill suddenly and collapsed in front of me," David told me. "It was not only my father but my whole world which collapsed before my eyes. The young instinctively refuse to accept death. My father was forty-five years older than I and was for me the symbol of the indestructible patriarch. He was both Moses and Louis Pasteur, perhaps also because he bore a striking resemblance to the scientist. I was his only son, and I knew he adored me. After all the fear and humiliation caused by the war, I again felt myself the victim of a terrible injustice."

His father's body was not even cold, David remembers, when dealers in antiques and paintings invaded the house buying up the Isabeys, the Louis XV commode, the Tiepolos, the bronze bust by Bologne, the Courbet, and David's treasured "Saint Sebastian." All were gobbled up at a fraction of their value.

After they had removed the paintings from the living room, David looked at the bare walls and the squares and rectangles etched in the old wallpaper. They infuriated him so that he took a box of school paints and tried to fill up the empty spaces with landscapes and still life.

David never forgot that impulsive, first attempt to paint what in effect was a mural or montage. He had never studied art to any great extent in school, and drawing classes, if you can believe that, bored him. Yet, as he told me, "The shapes and colors fell into a pattern all by themselves."

I think that spontaneous explosion by David after seeing those paintings—especially his revered "Saint Sebastian"—taken away from their places of honor in his house was the turning point in his life. He believes so, too.

"It was as if my paintbrush were possessed," I remember David telling me. "I felt a certain thrill at squeezing the tubes of gouache and blending the colors on a strip of cardboard. No, those were not *chefs-d'oeuvre*, and yet I know now that in a moment of exultation that afternoon I first experienced my overwhelming attraction to painting."

He had become a painter unwittingly. But those months following the death of his father were filled with turmoil and bitterness. He sought refuge in books. He spent days in his bed holding his head in his hands behind the locked door of his room until he was cramped with pain. And when the pain subsided, he went hungrily through Proust, Melville, Ezra Pound, and Jean Cocteau. Yet his favorite book always remained *The Portrait of Dorian Gray*. He was intrigued by Oscar Wilde as a person and by his cult of aestheticism.

Though David was unable to continue his studies at the conservatory because he had to work to support his mother, he nevertheless managed in a matter of months to enter the Sorbonne and take up the study of literature. David's natural talents at the keyboard enabled him to find work as a pianist in Paris nightclubs. He played mostly jazz because that was the most popular form of music in that environment then, as it still is now.

David completed the four-year degree course at the Sorbonne—with a brief period of study in England as well—and upon
graduation landed a job as a reporter with an evening newspaper
in Paris that has since become defunct. Later, David served as a
lieutenant in the French army. He did duty during the Algerian
war in Dakar, then in the Sahara Desert with a meharist (camel-
back) company based at Fort-Gouroud.

One afternoon the company commander looked around the
bare walls of the officers' mess and said, "It's awfully sad here."
He turned to David and asked if he knew how to paint. David
answered that he wasn't a painter but admitted that he had done
a few sketches in the past. His mind raced back to an earlier,
sadder time when he splashed the walls of his living room with
paints to hide the scars of heartbreak.

"We're not looking for Michelangelo," the company commander said. Then he showed David a magazine with color
prints of Tuareg frescoes which had recently been discovered in
the Hoggar Mountains of the desert. David was overwhelmed
with the beauty of the frescoes that depicted hunting and war
scenes. The simple lines and pure colors had a great affinity with
Egyptian art.

David told his commander he'd be willing to try to copy the
frescoes on the barren mess-hall walls. The army quartermaster
had only house paint. Then the thought came to David—the
artists who had done those frescoes had nothing more to work
with than clay, chalk, and ocher.

So David mounted a camel and headed for the hills to gather
different-colored soils. He packed them into his saddlebags,
brought them back to the base, mixed his pigments in mess ket-
tles, then went to work on the walls copying the Tuareg frescoes
from the magazine pages.

For a whole month, like Michelangelo, David was perched
on scaffolding and reproducing three ten-by-fifteen-foot frescoes.
With the sweat rolling down his bare back, he worked feverishly
through siesta time to take advantage of the bright midday light.
The soldiers gawked in astonishment at David's daily progress.

When his work was finished, the happy commander ordered a
barbecue in honor of the whole company. Commander and company were unanimous in their praise of David's work, and they

told him they found very little difference in the frescoes on the mess-hall walls and the ones that the Tuaregs did.

"Why the devil didn't you sign it?" the commander asked David.

"But it's the work of a great anonymous artist, sir," David responded. "Why should I be the one to sign it?"

That was David's first real attempt as an artist, and it certainly gave him something to think about.

It wasn't until he returned to Paris that David turned to art— and forgery—as a career. That occasion came about quite by accident. It came at a period of his life when he didn't know where he was heading.

"I was out every night and would wake up about three in the afternoon in some sordid hotel on the Left Bank," David told me. "Instinctively I kept returning to Saint-Germain-des-Prés, which was the only place in Paris where I didn't feel like a displaced person. I lived on cups of coffee and croissants, and most of all I nourished my hatred for a society which had no place for me."

David had begun to feel antagonistic toward the "establishment" during his days in the army. Even when he was doing the painting in the mess hall, he had to drop his brushes on many occasions and grab his Thompson submachine gun and dash off to the Moroccan border with his squad where the Algerian rebels were getting their supplies. The battles, which included ground support from the Spanish Bandera and air cover by the French air force, were sometimes bloody.

"I'm not ashamed to admit that I was scared and disgusted when I saw my fellow soldiers die at my side for a cause which I didn't really believe in," David has told me.

During his bleak period in Paris, thoughts of that war and its cruelties raced through David's mind. He thought of his own plight. He was going nowhere.

"Many times when I came home at dawn, I would feel myself overcome with the urge to commit suicide," I remember David telling me. "Lack of money haunted me. Middle-class morality made me sick. I had this awful feeling of being a talented misfit. I had reached a point of depression where I felt capable of everything—including the worst."

The David Stein who was living with me was in that same

frame of mind. In his condition as a drug addict David again felt that he was "capable of everything." But no matter how difficult things got, I never heard David mention doing "the worst."

It was while he was in this low state of mind that David met Marc, an old college friend, in the Montana Bar on the Rue St.-Benôit. David suddenly felt ashamed of his dirty shirt and jacket, which was too shiny at the elbows. He didn't even have enough money to buy Marc a drink.

"How have you been?" David asked.

"I'm mixed up in the art business," Marc replied rather vaguely.

"And what about you?" he asked, filling David's glass from his bottle of Scotch. David confessed he was right in the middle of nowhere and that he just couldn't get hold of himself.

Without a word, Marc slipped one hundred francs into David's pocket, and then they talked until six in the morning. David told Marc everything about his life in the Sahara, and when he mentioned that he had reproduced those frescoes, his listener suddenly became very interested.

"I might have something for you," Marc said. "Why don't you drop by at my hotel tomorrow around five."

The Louisiana Hotel was a refuge for foreigners, artists, jazz musicians, and all sorts of people who get along somehow. Marc lay stretched out on his bed in a polka-dot bathrobe. Magazines of all sorts, mostly on art, were scattered over the floor. A sticky-sweet odor of eau de cologne and Virginia tobacco, which for David was "a symbol of luxury," hung heavy in the room. Marc half-jokingly showed David a sketch by Cocteau which was in a nice frame.

"What do you think of it?" asked Marc. "You were a good friend of his."

David studied the drawing closely.

"I saw him do dozens of these," David finally told Marc.

"But you didn't see him do this one," Marc smiled.

"No," David answered.

Marc broke into laughter and jabbed David in the ribs.

"It was done by a young painter, a good friend of mine," Marc said. "Let me tell you, that sort of thing sells."

"Why are you telling me all this?" David asked in puzzlement.

Marc put his hands on David's shoulders and looked him straight in the eyes as if he were trying to hypnotize him.

"Because I know that you are talented and broke, and besides, you have seen Cocteau do it. How about giving it a try? What have you got to lose?"

As David told me, "Marc was absolutely right—I had nothing to lose."

They went downstairs to a café and ordered drinks. As they sipped from their glasses of cognac, David doodled with a pencil on a sheet of paper. Marc grabbed the sheet and exclaimed, "That's a Cocteau if I ever saw one. I bet we could sell it right now."

"Not on this paper," David smiled. He had made his sketch on the back of the menu.

"Well," Marc came back, "let us go and buy some good paper and materials, and we'll see whether you can't fool the world with your talents."

They bought pencils, India ink, pastels, and a book of Cocteau's drawings, then went back to the café and sought out a quiet corner. Marc opened the book at random, pointed to the page, and told David, "Try to do this one."

"*Magnifique!*" Marc cried as David finished the drawing. It had taken him a few minutes to complete the work. "You have captured the master's lucid style!"

"Why shouldn't I have?" David asked when he was telling me the story. "It was instinctive. After all, hadn't I been at Cocteau's side as I studied his graphic style? I merely gave life to something which was a part of me. And for that reason I didn't have the feeling that I was producing a fake."

Marc said he was going to sell the drawing immediately. He went to the phone, called an art gallery, and gave them the routine that he had just acquired a very rare drawing. The gallery owner asked him to bring it in.

David went with his friend but only as far as the door.

"You go in and try to sell it," David pleaded. "I am too scared."

Marc went. Minutes later he came out without the Cocteau. He was smiling. Instead of the Cocteau, Marc had five hundred francs in his hand—one hundred dollars!

"They were delighted with it," Marc said. "They want more."
And that is how David started as an art forger. . . .

Now it was less than four years later, and David had painted
and sketched literally thousands of forgeries, not only Cocteaus
but Chagalls, Picassos, Van Dongens, Derains, Dufys, Braques,
and Marie Laurencins. And where had all this effort gotten him?

We were living in our summer of discontent. We were in the
lap of luxury, and yet we were deeply in debt and without any
hope of emancipating ourselves from our mounting obligations
because of David's free-wheeling spending habits.

David was still on his five-a-day drug kick, still irritable and
impossible to live with, and on top of all that I was suddenly
faced with another challenge. David's mother was coming from
Paris to visit us!

19

DAVID'S MOTHER
BRINGS BAD LUCK

More than anything, David wanted to impress his mother. There was no question in my mind that Mrs. Haddad—now Madame Leonne Gast, for she had married again—would be impressed with our sumptuous apartment on Park Avenue, which was as elegant as anything Paris had to offer. And I was certain she would be impressed with David's Silver Cloud Rolls Royce, which was driven as usual by his chauffeur that afternoon in early September when we went to Kennedy Airport to meet his mother.

But David had to make an even bigger impression on his *maman*, so he went out and bought a twelve-hundred-dollar mink stole—not for me, but for her. It didn't bother me that he had bought her that mink; I admired his sentiment. But there we were, virtually bankrupt, and he was adding to our debt.

David's mother did not look anything like what I had pictured her to be. I had never seen a photo of her, and David had never described her to me. So when I saw a short, slender woman with brown hair who looked more like fifty than sixty-five, I was rather surprised. I had visions of a completely different looking person, perhaps taller, gray-haired, and much older looking.

David and his mother had a warm, affectionate reunion. They embraced and kissed just as mother and son should after a separation of nearly four years. But her greeting to me was a non-committal handshake. Well, after all, we *were* strangers, even though I had borne her son a daughter, and was now pregnant with our second child. I had no right to feel slighted if her greeting was cool, because this was her big moment with her son.

But what of Cecilia—her granddaughter—whom we had brought with us to the airport? Didn't this cherubic, smiling, dimpled doll of a girl who had just passed her first birthday deserve more than a passing glance? I was holding Ceci in my arms, and the only notice she received from her grandmother was a half-smile. Not a word of endearment.

I wasn't yet prepared to dislike David's mother, because I excused her aloofness to me and the baby as owing to the tiring eight hours she had spent in the air. But that evening when David took his mother and me to dine at Le Mistral, one of New York's finest French restaurants, I saw the true nature of the woman. She was heartless.

David and his mother were reminiscing about the early, happy days, when his father was alive. Suddenly David asked his mother, "Tell me frankly, *maman*, which of your three husbands did you like best?"

David's mother seemed to stiffen. Her face became hard. She tightened her lips. Then she answered her son.

"Oh, David, if you want to know the truth, the only reason I married your father was because I had to feed three children. . . ."

As her voice faded, I turned in paralyzed shock and disgust to study David's reaction. Tears were trickling down his cheeks. It was the first time I had seen David cry.

"How can you say something like that?" David said in a choked voice.

"It happens to be the truth," David's mother responded gruffly. "Living with your father was hell for me. He never paid me any attention. All he did was work, work, work. And those hours he kept drove me crazy. . . ."

The conversation ended soon after, David paid the check, and we took his mother to the Mayflower Hotel, where David and I had decided in advance to put her up so that she could enjoy her own privacy. Our apartment had no sleeping accommodations for guests except for a convertible couch in the den.

It was several days before David warmed up to his mother again. He barely spoke to her at lunch and dinner, which we ate alternately at our apartment and in various restaurants. In the meantime, I tried to maintain a civil rapport with Madame Gast, who out of respect to David I called *maman*. Dutifully every day I walked to the hotel, picked her up, and took her shopping and visiting friends like the Kramers, the Wolkenbergs, and the Lublins.

While I was entertaining or catering to his mother during the day, David was busy selling Chagalls. He had just pulled one of his bigger deals. He had sold three Chagall forgeries to Irving Yamet, an art dealer who had once been a partner of Abe Lublin. Now Yamet was on his own. His dealings with David had begun some six months earlier when he had bought a Giacometti drawing for two thousand dollars. It was a legitimate work that David had acquired from Paris.

But in recent times Yamet was mainly in the market for Chagalls, and the only person who was able to supply him with this master's works at reasonable cost was David. They were forgeries, and that was why the price was reasonable. Besides, David was desperate for money. He also knew that Yamet didn't want to pay the twelve- and fifteen-thousand-dollar figures that other dealers or galleries were demanding for the available Chagalls, which were the painter's larger works.

Yamet wanted smaller pieces that sold for five and six thousand. David had plenty of these in our apartment, for before his mother had arrived in New York, he had produced about a dozen in preparation for a big killing with Yamet, who had been bugging David for months to get him Chagalls.

I'll never forget the day. It was September 10, in the afternoon. The doorbell rang, and I opened the door and saw Yamet, whom I knew quite well, since we had had him over for dinner.

"Is David home?" he asked in a calm voice.

I escorted Yamet inside and called David.

Yamet greeted David warmly and then stated his reason for being there.

"Those last three Chagalls that you sold me," Yamet said, "will require authentication."

"Authentication?" David asked, nonplussed. He had sold Yamet three other Chagalls earlier, and there had been no such request. Why did Yamet want proof now that the works were legitimate?

"Because the party I am selling them to demands it," Yamet explained. "You can get it quite easily, can't you, David?" he asked.

"Oh, of course," David said with a sweep of his hand. "Without any trouble. All I have to do is write to Paris."

But that wasn't as easy as it sounded. It would have been extremely simple if the Chagalls were real. But how do you get an expert to validate a Chagall forgery? If David were to have sent photos of the works he had created to one of the several art experts in Paris who judge such paintings, there is no way of knowing whether he would have stamped his approval on the back of the photos, which is all that is required to prove authenticity.

Yet, since all that's needed is that stamp on the back of a photo, the problem of proving that his fakes were legitimate was not insurmountable. In fact, it was easy. David had anticipated the possibility of being asked to produce such proof at one time or another, especially since he had become involved in selling Chagalls exclusively.

To prepare himself for that contingency, David had had his own stamp forged about a month before. He had used the name of one of Paris's better-known art experts, André Pacitti. Getting Pacitti's stamp made was quite simple. David merely went to a printing firm specializing in rubber stamps. He posed as Pacitti and told them that he was on a business trip to New York and had lost his valued rubber stamp. He showed the printer an imprint on the back of a legitimate Chagall photo that bore Pacitti's stamp, and the printer promptly made an identical replica.

As you already are aware, David was desperate for money. Yamet had three of his Chagalls which commanded ten thousand dollars. If David could produce proof of their authenticity, he would be paid. Now that David had the wherewithal to show that proof, he went about doing so immediately.

On September 12, just two days after Yamet had visited us, David phoned the dealer and told him that he had just received the authenticating papers from Paris.

"Bring them to me," Yamet said. David did. Then that night came the rude awakening. We were sitting in the living room relaxing after a night out with his mother. Suddenly David bolted upright in his chair.

"*Chérie*," he cried, "I made a big mistake! I think we might be in trouble."

"Trouble?" I said with an air of unconcern. With our financial condition being what it was and with David on drugs, I couldn't imagine what else there could be to worry about, except another bill, another call from the bank, another outburst by David.

"I gave Yamet the authenticating papers too soon," he said.

I didn't understand.

"Don't you see?" he asked. "Yamet was here two days ago for authentication. I told him I was going to write to Paris for it. And here I have already delivered it to him. Mail never travels that fast between Paris and New York. . . ."

David's voice dropped off. He was genuinely frightened, and his fear was heightened because he did not trust Yamet. I had never seen David like that before. That night I don't think he slept more than an hour, but his lack of sleep did not dull his thinking. In the morning he had a plan prepared to bail out if Yamet had realized the impossible speed with which authentication had come from Paris.

David had uncanny intuition, and his divination of Yamet was that Yamet was not a man to give a swindler an even break. And although David realized that he was defrauding his buyers, he always looked to them for an even break. He was convinced that most of the people with whom he dealt would give him a chance to offer an explanation if they discovered that he had sold them a forgery. He felt the worst that could happen would be that the buyer of the fake would ask for his money back, and David was always prepared to return it. But he didn't feel that Yamet would react to a swindle in that manner.

"He is the kind of man who will run to the authorities," David told me that morning of the thirteenth. "I am very afraid he will make trouble."

Now came his plan.

"*Chérie*," David said, "I want you to pack up all the evidence—the paintings, the paints, the paper, the stamp, everything. I know the first thing the authorities will do is search the apartment. If they find nothing, they cannot accuse me of anything more serious than selling fake paintings. And I can always say I didn't know they were fake and that I was duped myself when I bought them."

I followed David's instructions to the letter. I packed everything in the apartment that represented evidence of his involvement in art forgery. The evidence filled a large suitcase, which I left in the den. That afternoon David was to take the suitcase over to his doctor's house for safe storage. That was the least the doctor could do for David after all the money he had made off him.

With the packing out of the way, David and I settled down to a normal routine. I went to the Mayflower and took David's mother shopping. That evening we dined at home, as we did the following evening, the fifteenth.

I remember distinctly that I had cooked beef Bourguignon and that we were in the middle of it when the doorbell rang. David got up to answer. It was Yamet.

"I've got to talk to you," I heard him say. David led him into the living room to wait for us to finish dinner and returned to the table.

"What does he want?" I asked.

"He didn't tell me," David said. He looked relieved. He didn't say anything because his mother was at the table, but I assumed that next to the worst had happened—Yamet had detected the fraud but had not done what David had feared he might do. Instead of going to the authorities, he came to our apartment to give David the "even break" he had always expected from his victims.

But during dinner I became uneasy. So did David. Every now and then we caught a glimpse of Yamet peeking in the dining room. It was as though he were spying on us. He seemed anxious—even fidgety. I couldn't understand why.

The doorbell rang again, and this time we were startled. David rose slowly from his seat at the table and went to answer it—a glass of champagne in his hand. I had my eyes fixed on David. He looked through the peephole, as he and I always did before opening the door. I saw him bolt back, turn, take quick steps toward the service door just off the dining area, wheel around, and signal me to come over.

"My mother always brought me bad luck," David whispered. "Good-bye, *chérie*. . . ."

And with that, David went out the service door, the glass of champagne still in his hand.

I didn't know what he was talking about until the doorbell rang again, and I went to see who was there. When I put my eye to the peephole, I knew why David had made his hurried exit. I saw two familiar faces—Assistant District Attorney Joseph Stone and Detective Nick Barrett!

My first thought was to give David all the time possible to escape. I didn't open the door. I went back to the table and sat down. The bell rang again. I didn't get up to answer. But Irving Yamet came out of the living room and went to the door.

I leaped up, rushed over to Yamet, who had his hand on the doorknob, and screamed, "You have a hell of a nerve!"

He snickered at me as he opened the door to admit Stone, Barrett, and several other district attorney's detectives. I am certain Yamet had convinced the prosecutor's office that David deserved to be arrested.

I had always hoped that David would never be caught at his game. But suddenly now, with the district attorney's squad in our house and trying to enter the locked door of our den, I was almost wishing that David would be arrested. How else could I feel? Beyond that door lay all the evidence that Stone and his sleuths needed to hang David. The suitcase that I had packed with David's paper, paints, paintings, and forged stamp was still there. David had forgotten to take it to his doctor's house!

20

ESCAPE—BUT ONLY A
COUNTDOWN TO DISASTER

The district attorney's detectives had taken every precaution to thwart David's escape. They had posted civilian-clad sleuths in the lobby and service entrances.

Since David had made his bid for freedom down the service entrance, it was obvious that he would be collared by the detective staked out there. But there was a slight hitch, or oversight, in the lawmen's strategy. The detective had his eye on the service elevator, and David had used the stairs.

As I learned later from David, he managed on tiptoes to skirt neatly around the detective's back, because the detective had his eyes fixed on the service-elevator door. But David's flight wasn't all that easy. Beyond the service entrance-exit was a six-foot-high wrought-iron spiked fence with a gate. The gate was padlocked for the night. So David scaled the fence, rushed to the Lexington Avenue subway, and made his way downtown to the Bowery, where he sought refuge in a flophouse.

Upstairs on the eighth floor, I was frantic as Stone and Barrett confronted me.

"Where is David?" Stone demanded.

"I don't know," I replied, which was the truth.

"He was here a minute ago," shouted Yamet.

Then he tried to lead Stone and the other investigators around the apartment in what I detected was an attempt by Yamet to conduct a search. As he started into the bedroom I screamed, "Don't you go in there!" Then I protested to Stone that Yamet had no business in the apartment. Indeed, I told the prosecutor that even he and his detectives had no right to be there.

"Do you have a search warrant?" I demanded.

Stone said they had, but it was with a detective downstairs.

"Let me see it," I said.

A detective was dispatched to get the document. When it was shown to me, I stepped back and said, "Go ahead with your search."

My heart was pounding. What would I say when the investigators asked to enter the locked den, where all the evidence needed to incriminate David as an art forger was stuffed in that tightly packed suitcase that would never have been there if David had not goofed?

Before Stone and his men started their search, I put up another protest.

"I don't want Yamet in here," I shouted. "Get him out! Get him out!"

Yamet was asked to leave.

Now I had another problem to contend with—David's mother. The confusion of the last few minutes had confounded her, and she was wandering around the living room in a state of disorientation. I went to her, took her by the arm, led her into the bedroom where Cecilia was asleep in her crib, and said, "*Maman*, you stay in here." Then I closed the door.

The bedroom, kitchen, and dining room were given a thorough search, but they yielded nothing that interested the investigators. But the foyer and living room were something else again. We had some 60 paintings hanging on the walls, and Stone ordered his men to remove every one of them. We had another 50 unframed paintings filed in a blueprint cabinet in the foyer. Those were taken, too. All 110 paintings were legitimate works of art. There wasn't a David Stein forgery among them.

In fact, there wasn't a fake in the whole apartment, but I don't believe that is what Stone was thinking when he finally approached the locked den and asked me to open the door. I unlocked it, and the detectives swarmed inside to continue their search. As I stood at the door watching them, I couldn't help but wonder why they were ignoring the suitcase that I had placed in a corner of the room. They passed it by time and again without even so much as a glance. Were they going to overlook this most significant evidence? I was hoping they would, but they didn't. One detective eventually picked up the suitcase, placed it on a table, and opened it.

"What have we here?" Stone asked.

I walked over, glanced at the contents, then looked at the prosecutor with a demure smile.

"They are my art supplies," I said. "I paint as a hobby. Is that a crime?"

"Take it downtown with the rest of the stuff," Stone ordered his detectives. Then he turned to me.

"Mrs. Stein," he said, "we are looking for your husband. If you know where he is, I wish you would tell me. It will be a lot easier on him if he gives himself up; we are not going to stop looking for him. Please tell him that when you hear from him."

It was shortly before midnight when Stone and the detectives departed. I could tell by the expressions on their faces that they were greatly disappointed over the outcome of their mission. They had come there to arrest David and were ever so certain that they would find him. In fact, as I learned later, Yamet had been sent to our apartment for just that purpose—to establish that David was there. The prearranged signal for the raid was the time element. If Yamet had not found David in, he would have gone downstairs to inform the raiders. By remaining upstairs for more than fifteen minutes, the detectives would know David was home, and all they had to do was come upstairs and arrest him. To this day I feel Yamet was more put out than anyone else that David gave him and the sleuths the slip. Although David had escaped, it was not really a flight to freedom. As I look back on that episode, it was only a countdown to disaster.

That night I didn't sleep. For the first time in months, I rolled the TV set out of our bedroom closet and watched the late-hour movies until dawn. During the following day I paced the apartment frantic with worry about David. I didn't expect him to phone because I'm certain he suspected our lines were tapped.

The only way David could get word to me of his whereabouts would be through a friend. But what friend? I couldn't know. We hadn't prepared for a crisis like this. All I could do was wait. It was a long wait. Time went slowly that day of the sixteenth.

As if I didn't have enough to worry about, I had David's mother around my neck night and day. She refused to go back to her hotel until she saw David. What a woman!

"Anne-Marie," she kept repeating, "why did you let this happen during my visit? You have spoiled my whole trip. David is just like his father . . . thoughtless."

She was blaming me as though I had scheduled the prosecutor's raid during her visit. And she was showing her true colors as a mother. What I wanted to do now more than anything else was to get that gorgon out of our apartment and back to Paris. But I couldn't put her on the plane until I had heard from David. Two days had gone by and still no word from him.

The seventeenth dawned with renewed hope in my heart that I would hear from David. I also awakened from a troubled sleep with a firm resolve to correct a grave wrong. I left David's mother to baby-sit with Cecilia and went on an urgent errand. When I returned, I was confronted immediately by Madame Gast.

"Where is my mink stole?" she almost shrieked. "It isn't here!"

I pretended to know nothing about it. My act didn't fool her.

"I know you have it! I know you've taken it!" she screamed. "I want it back!"

I was hoping she would shut up and forget the stole. But she wouldn't. She was driving me crazy. Finally I let her have it.

"You are the most obnoxious woman I have ever met!" I yelled. "You are selfish and self-centered. You don't give a damn about anyone—not your son, not your granddaughter, no one. You are a vulture!"

I stopped to catch my breath and take stock of her reaction. She was glaring at me in stupefaction. Then I told her what had happened to her fur piece.

"We can't afford to pay for that stole, and I have taken it back to the store," I said. "Now the next thing I am going to do is get rid of you. Go back to the hotel and pack your things. You are going back to Paris."

Muttering under her breath, she walked out of the apartment. I then phoned a girl friend and asked her to meet David's mother at the Mayflower.

"Just take her to Kennedy Airport and make sure she gets on a plane to Paris," I said.

A few hours later the friend called. Mission accomplished.

More hours passed. My concern for David was greater than ever. Where had he gone? Why hadn't he gotten in touch? I could no longer stand it. I knew that there was one friend among all the ones we had who'd be the most likely to hear from David with a message for me. I decided to call him. I went downstairs to a pay phone, because I didn't want to call from the apartment.

"Anne-Marie," he said. "Just this minute I heard from David. He is all right. He is at the Sheraton Hotel. He wants me to bring him some money because he is going to Philadelphia."

David was going there to stay with another friend. And the message, which was to be delivered to me in person because David felt the police would be listening in on our phone, was: Pack our belongings and wait for his doctor to pick up Cecilia and me. David had made arrangements with the doctor to take us to his home in Scarsdale, a fashionable suburb just north of the New York City line.

Although I had despised the doctor because of his indiscriminate administration of drugs to David, I had never shown any outward animosity toward him. I think I hid my feelings pretty well. Our relationship had always been friendly—and at a time like this I couldn't be choosy about people who wanted to help David and me.

After I had packed our belongings, the doctor and his wife drove Cecilia and me to their home, where we stayed a week. It was a tense, nervous week for me. David was on the phone from Philadelphia every day.

"Everything will be all right," he kept assuring me. "I am making arrangements to take you and Ceci away. Keep the suitcases packed because I may be there anytime."

Near midnight on the seventh day, September 25, the bell rang. The maid opened the door. It was David. I rushed over and threw my arms around him.

"We are going," he said.

The car in which David arrived was driven by the friend in Philadelphia. He took us on a forty-five-minute journey to Hoboken, New Jersey, just across the Hudson River from Manhattan. We stayed at the Renaissance Motel, which was the least commodious lodging David and I had paused at since our furnished-room days in Paris. But fugitives can't be choosy.

In the morning the friend drove us to Asbury Park, a seaside resort on the south Jersey coast, where David had rented a house that was owned by a John Bircher who gave us an American flag when we moved in.

I found the off-season quiet of Asbury Park a welcome tonic after our hectic, hair-raising adventures of the last fortnight. I was in the eighth month of my pregnancy now, and my concern about where I was going to have my baby was heightening daily. But David kept assuring me that we would soon go "somewhere far away."

Our stay in Asbury Park was to last only until David had received the four thousand dollars he had paid as a deposit on another store he had rented in Palm Beach for an art gallery for the 1966–67 season. Now, of course, with District Attorney Hogan in pursuit of David, those plans were scrubbed. The friend in Philadelphia, who knew the landlord of the building well, was trying to break the lease and get David's deposit back. We needed that money desperately to put miles between us and the bloodhounds.

Near the end of our second week on the Jersey shore, the friend arrived with the money in cash. It was our ticket to a freedom that neither David nor I was foolish enough to believe could last long. We expected the law to catch us sooner or later, but we also lived with the outside hope that we might make our escape permanent.

David had a long-range plan. He wanted to go to Mexico, but not before I had the baby. I was still a month or so away from giving birth. We both wanted the baby to be born in the United States, because we felt its medical facilities were better than what we might find south of the border. Moreover, I wanted my second-born to be an American citizen as Cecilia was.

With the four thousand dollars in hand we were ready to travel. The friend drove us to the Newark Station of the Pennsylvania Railroad, where David bought two one-way tickets to San Francisco. Because Cecilia was an infant, she rode the pullman free. We arrived in Chicago just before noon of the next day. We had something like a five-hour layover before our next train, the Burlington Route's *Zephyr*, would whisk us westward to our destination.

David and I decided to while away the time browsing through Marshall Field's department store. It was a bitter-cold day, and we almost froze. We had worn warm-weather clothing when we left Asbury Park and knew nothing about how cold it gets in the Midwest, let alone the fact that we would be changing trains in Chicago. We had thought crossing the continent was a continuous ride.

I enjoyed the second half of our journey much more than the first part. The scenery was breathtaking. I had never seen anything to match the beauty of the Rockies. I felt the same way when we arrived in San Francisco. What a glorious city! Except when the fog rolls in. That chilled me to the bone and caused me to lose my fascination and appreciation of its Old World charm.

We took a room in a modest hotel on Market Street a short distance from the fashionable San Franciscan. Our limited funds had finally braked David's extravagance. As it was, the room was costing us nearly thirty-five dollars a day. Our first thought was to find a furnished apartment. But finding one was not all that easy. In San Francisco, it seems, nobody wants to rent to people with children. It took us two weeks to rent a flat. It was on Twin Peaks Hill and afforded a magnificent view of the bay overlooking Oakland—when we weren't fogged in.

One of my foremost concerns after we moved was to prepare for the birth of my baby. More than anything I had to have a doctor. And since we didn't know anyone in San Francisco who could recommend one, I let my fingers walk the yellow pages until I found Dr. Donald DeCarle with offices in the downtown section.

I made an appointment and went to see him. I didn't take a cab, which was my accustomed way of getting places, because it was too rich for my blood. I rode the trolley—and really enjoyed it.

Dr. DeCarle found me in excellent condition except for my

blood pressure, which was extremely low. He prescribed as much rest as possible. He also had what I thought was a wonderful bedside manner. He knew how to buoy a prospective mother whose mental attitude in the face of recent events had hit rock bottom.

"You're going to have a boy, and he'll weigh eight pounds," DeCarle said.

I took the trolley home but felt as if I were sailing on a high cloud—that's how much my spirits had been elevated. But my mood soon took a downturn in that dreary flat. David's frame of mind did a lot to diminish my newfound cheerfulness. David was despondent because now, for the first time since his aimless days in Paris, he didn't know when the next dollar would come in.

After our cross-country train trip, two weeks spent in the Market Street hotel, all the eating-out during that period, and the three months' deposit we gave for the apartment, the four thousand dollars that we had started with had dwindled to a paltry seven hundred. David wasn't only despondent; he was desperate.

"So many galleries in San Francisco," David began saying. "If I could only paint. . . ."

I almost had the baby in the middle of the room.

"Don't you dare try that!" I raged at him. "You will get caught, and that will be the last time I see you. Every gallery in the country must be on the lookout for you. Please, David, promise me you won't do anything so foolish."

David promised, but I didn't believe him. I knew that he had no other means of making money now than doing what came naturally—painting forgeries. And I knew we would soon need money to pay the doctor and the hospital, not to mention the clothes and other needs I would have to buy for the baby. I felt certain that David would try to rip off a few Chagalls or Van Dongens behind my back and unload them on some gallery in town. I kept my eyes on him like a hawk. I even searched through the closets and drawers whenever David went shopping for food to make certain he hadn't smuggled in paper and pastels to do his paintings in the middle of the night when I was asleep.

But David remained true to his word. He spent every day and most of every evening watching TV.

Five days after Thanksgiving, on Tuesday, November 29, I

awakened at 8 A.M. My first inclination was to dress and prepare for my noon appointment with Dr. DeCarle. But no sooner had I gotten on my feet than I realized that I wouldn't be seeing the doctor in his office, but in the hospital. Those familiar labor pains had started.

I awakened David, who dressed and took Cecilia down the block to a couple who had a daughter her age and had agreed to care for our little girl when I went into the hospital. When David returned, I was ready. And so was the cab, which David had summoned before picking me up. It was our first taxi ride in San Francisco.

Everything happened quickly once I was admitted to Children's Hospital. I was taken upstairs in a wheelchair, undressed, wheeled into the labor room, given a spinal, and in seconds I was completely numb from the waist down. I had told Dr. DeCarle that I wanted to be awake and see my baby being delivered.

Not many minutes passed and I was in the delivery room. Things didn't go too well for a while.

"His head is turned," I heard Dr. DeCarle saying.

A nurse moved in closer.

"Forceps," the doctor called out.

The nurse handed them to him.

I couldn't feel a thing, but I could see they were struggling, trying to grasp the head. Presently, the movement by the doctor and nurse told me that everything was proceeding normally. When I saw the baby, I knew everything was all right.

Dr. DeCarle held the baby by the feet. I watched him slap his backside and heard the cry. It was like a kitten's muted meow. Then, still holding my little *bébé*, the doctor turned to me, smiling.

"I told you it was going to be a boy, didn't I?" he said.

But the doctor guessed wrong on the weight. Little Frédéric tipped the scale at only seven pounds nine ounces. DeCarle was off by a whole seven ounces.

David was true to form. He had disappeared from the hospital the instant he had brought me there. David had a real aversion to hospitals because they saddened him. I didn't hear from him until that evening when he phoned me in my semiprivate room.

"*Chérie*," he said, "I hear it's a boy. That's wonderful, isn't it?"

I wanted to know where he was. He told me he was with the couple who were caring for Cecilia.

"But aren't you going to visit me and see your son?" I asked.

"Right away," David answered.

A half hour later David was sitting beside me and telling me how proud he was that we had had a son.

"He is a beautiful boy," David said.

"How can you say that?" I told David. "He is ugly. Have you seen that big head and those horrible forceps marks?"

"He is still a beautiful boy," David insisted.

My first two days in the hospital were uneventful. David visited me again on the second night, and then returned on the third night pale as a ghost.

"What is wrong, David?" I asked, alarmed by his appearance.

"You will never believe what happened," he said tensely. "Yesterday I drew three Cocteaus, and I sold them to the Verdi Gallery. They agreed to pay me three hundred dollars and told me to come back for the money today. When I went there, what do you think happened? That man at the gallery said to me, 'Hello, David.'"

"And what was wrong with that?" I asked.

"But I had told him my name was Michael Harcourt," David said. He was shaking.

"Then how did he find out your name?" I wanted to know.

"I'll tell you," David said. "The minute he mentioned my name I started to run. Just as I got to the door, I spotted Yamet standing in a corner. I knew that son of a bitch exposed me."

As I was to learn later, David had been uncovered quite by accident. Yamet had come to San Francisco on a business trip and had dropped into the Verdi Gallery just minutes after David had sold his three Cocteau drawings. Yamet saw the sketches and asked the gallery owner where he had obtained them. The answer was from a Michael Harcourt.

That reply might have ended the conversation had it not been for the gallery owner's propensity for colloquy. In the ensuing interchange the gallery owner told Yamet that the man who had sold him the three Cocteaus was French—and that his wife had just given birth.

Yamet didn't have to put two and two together. He already had not a suspicion but a conviction that David Stein had unloaded the three Cocteaus on the Verdi Gallery. And he did not hesitate to pass on his conviction to the gallery owner. Nor waste any time calling District Attorney Hogan's office in New York.

During this time both David and I were unaware of a San Francisco detective who had come to Children's Hospital looking for me. The district attorney's office in New York knew it was close to my time to have the baby, and they had requested this detective to check the city's hospitals. The detective went to maternity, checked the records, then left. He didn't find me listed, because I was admitted under the name of Ann Harcourt. He was looking for Anne-Marie Stein.

If he had only asked the nurse in charge if she had any patient in maternity who spoke with a French accent, he would have found me. And if he had waited in my room he could have arrested David when he visited me.

David's divination of Yamet had been correct—he was not about to give a swindler a break. However, during my convalescence neither David nor I had imagined the extent to which Yamet had become involved with our lives and David's forged Chagalls. Yamet had become suspicious when the authentication from Paris was brought to him by David too quickly—on September 12.

On the afternoon of September 15, the afternoon preceding David's escape, Yamet informed the district attorney's office of his suspicions. He was asked to bring downtown those Chagalls he suspected were fakes to the prosecutor's frauds bureau. A quick call was made to a very distinguished visitor to the city— Marc Chagall himself, who had arrived for the mural dedication at the Metropolitan Opera. The artist agreed to let himself be escorted by a prosecutor's aide to the frauds bureau to look at the paintings in question.

When Chagall looked at them, he went into a rage.

"They are fakes!" he screamed, the vessels in his face ready to burst. "An outrage! Where did you get this garbage. It is terrible—terrible! I want them destroyed!"

He tried to tear the paintings, but Assistant District Attorney Stone and others in the room restrained him.

"This is evidence, Mr. Chagall," Stone said.

Chagall's histrionics were a little much, I thought, when the story was related to me. By protesting too much Chagall paid my husband the highest tribute. For if the paintings were all that bad, why should that concern Chagall? Any art dealer or gallery owner would recognize the fakery at once. But Irving Yamet, a supposedly experienced dealer, didn't recognize David's Chagalls as fakes. Neither did his former partner, Abe Lublin.

And I doubt that Chagall himself recognized the differences from his work—except that he knew he himself had never done those particular paintings.

"I must take you out of the hospital tonight," David said. "The situation is very critical."

I agreed. Fortunately, Dr. DeCarle had signed me out for the next morning, and San Francisco's Children's Hospital had no objection when I told them I wanted to leave that night. Frédéric was bundled into a blanket, and after I had dressed, he was put in my arms, and we were taken downstairs in a wheelchair. David had a cab waiting, which took us home.

We stayed no longer than it took us to pack. David called another cab at 8:30 P.M., and it got us to the station in plenty of time to catch the 10:00 train out of San Francisco to Los Angeles.

21

LIMOUSINE

TO CAPTURE

When we arrived at Union Station the next morning, David culled the yellow pages for a hotel, then called a cab that took us to our destination. I don't remember the name of the hotel, but I know it was just off Wilshire Boulevard. David found an apartment by scanning the classified section of the Los Angeles *Times*, and we moved out of the hotel almost as soon as we had registered.

We went to live in a darling furnished ground-floor apartment in Century City with a lovely patio-garden. What made the place even more inviting was the consideration we received from the Goldbergs, the landlord and his wife. They took David's word that he was expecting money from New York and not only rented us the apartment without a deposit but also loaned David a hundred dollars. Mrs. Goldberg even phoned the credit office of the Broadway Department Store, vouched for us, and we were able to buy essentials for the apartment and clothes for baby Frédéric on the easy-payment plan.

If the Goldbergs and other folks we met in Los Angeles did not happen to recognize us during the month we lived there, it was because we did not use our real names. We were known as Philip and Anne Gray, just as we had been Michael and Anne Harcourt in San Francisco. To this day, the records of the San Francisco Health Department still reflect those names on our son's birth certificate—Frédéric Harcourt. To change my son's name to Stein on his birth certificate necessitates my making an application in person in a San Francisco court, which I have not been able to do as yet.

The hundred-dollar loan from the Goldbergs went a long way toward helping launch David on a new spree of forgery which enabled us to get back on our feet. David bought paper and art supplies and promptly began turning out Van Dongens, Dufys, Marie Laurencins, Derains, and Cocteaus. But no Chagalls. The art world was by now alert to David's propensity for forging Chagalls, and all the art galleries were on the lookout.

Moreover, because David was such a wanted man, he couldn't chance showing his face at Los Angeles's art galleries to sell his forged works. So that became my job once again.

I had huge success with my first sale of a dozen small Cocteau profiles. And what a snow job I gave the owner of the gallery on Santa Monica Boulevard.

First I walked by the gallery and looked inside to make certain there were no familiar faces, and then I walked in with my sales pitch all rehearsed. I told the owner that my husband worked for one of the movie studios and that he and a group of associates were planning to produce a major film.

"We are trying to scrape together every cent we can get," I told the man, "and that is why I am here trying to sell these Cocteaus. I really don't want to part with them, and neither does my husband. But circumstances are forcing us to get rid of them."

I walked out after a nice quick sale with two hundred dollars in my pocketbook. Before I left, I had told the man that we had a few pieces at home that were "a little more expensive." He was interested.

"Bring them in and let me look at them," he said.

A few days later I returned to the gallery with a Dufy watercolor, a Van Dongen pastel and gouache, and a Derain gouache. The owner looked at the paintings admiringly and offered me seventeen hundred dollars.

"I guess that's all right," I said. "We're still trying to raise the money for that movie, and this will help. . . ."

After the owner wrote out the check to Anne Gray, I said, "We have a couple more pieces at home, and if we must sell them, I will bring them to you for first refusal."

He seemed pleased with my loyalty to his gallery. And I had every intention of returning there for another quick sale and even looked forward to selling many more of David's fakes to other galleries in the Los Angeles area. I was feeling animated and eager to pursue my role as David's *courtière* inasmuch as he couldn't show his face at the galleries.

I'm certain the environment (the smog notwithstanding) made me feel that way. I loved the warm, sunny climate, and I was elated by the warmth and friendliness of the people. There was a marked contrast between the denizens of this sprawling metropolis and those I met in San Francisco, who are aloof and sometimes as chilly as the fog that rolls into that city.

David also felt rejuvenated. I guess the improvement he saw in me made him feel better. And little Frédéric seemed to bring a new closeness to David and me that we had not known since pre–Palm Beach days. But most of all, I think, David was responsible for the change in me and in himself. The harrowing events of our last fortnight in New York, beginning with the district attorney's raid on our apartment, brought David out of his megalomaniac trauma. He came to realize he was not the "untouchable" he thought he was. David's encounter with Yamet in San Francisco gave him even more pause to think and make a full return to his senses. Of course, the fact that he had stopped taking drugs also helped immeasurably.

Well, there we were in Los Angeles. Almost back to normal, almost like old times. David forging. Anne-Marie selling. Oh, what a beautiful arrangement. Now, if only prosecutor Stone's sleuths and Yamet the headhunter would stay out of our lives, we could sell enough fakes to finance our flight from the United States.

Just thinking about it made me feel great. Even while I was getting the diapers ready for the washing machine that night of January 20, 1967, I was counting our blessings and numbering the days until David and I could take Cecilia and Frédéric to Mexico and start a new life.

It was dark when I started across the patio-garden for the laundry room. But I had never been afraid of darkness, and I gave no thought to it that night. In fact, my mind at that moment was on the sight-seeing trips we had been taking the last several days. With money coming in from the sale of David's paintings, we were beginning to enjoy some modest luxuries. All our excursions were taken in a hired, chauffeur-driven limousine. That might sound extravagant, but the limousine did not cost us any more than what we would have paid a cab driver to drive us around to all the places we had wanted to see.

It had never occurred to David or me that this innocent routine could get us in trouble. After all, we were using an alias. How could New York detectives who lost our trail in San Francisco ever pick it up again, when they didn't have the foggiest notion that we were masquerading as Philip and Anne Gray?

I found out after a terrifying moment on the garden patio, when two pairs of arms reached out of the darkness and enveloped my body. I stifled an outcry when I heard a husky voice say, "New York police."

They shoved me unceremoniously through the open door leading to our kitchen, and in the light I saw my captors—two burly Irish-faced detectives whom I'd seen before. They were members of the team that invaded our Park Avenue apartment-gallery.

"Where's David?" one of them asked.

"Look for yourself," I snapped.

They looked and quickly found him. David was in his pajamas in the bedroom—calmly painting a Marie Laurencin.

The detectives allowed David to put on his street clothes in the bathroom after they checked the narrow casement window and satisfied themselves that their prisoner couldn't squeeze through.

"Au revoir, chérie," David said as the detectives led him out. "I hope to see you again."

The next day I visited David in the police headquarters jail.

"Do you know how they traced us?" David shook his head mournfully. "The detectives checked the limousine services because they knew that we always rode in style back in New York."

"But how could they trace us when we were using the name Gray?" I asked.

"They were pretty smart. They asked the limousine people whether they had picked up a couple with a French accent with a little girl a year and a half old and a baby." I had to admit they *were* pretty smart.

I saw David again the next day, and by then he was ready to give in. I had gotten an attorney—through the yellow pages—to represent him, and he had been ready to fight extradition. But David decided there was no point to that. He agreed to return to New York.

On January 21, 1967, the two detectives took David to the airport and flew back to New York, first-class. I flew back with Cecilia and Frédéric economy class, but not as effortlessly as David and the district attorney's men. I could kick David for not having imposed a condition on his waiver of extradition. He should have demanded, "I won't go back unless you fly my wife and children to New York." But he didn't, and I was left to fend for myself.

I packed the children's and my belongings into six large suitcases and called a cab. When we got to the airport, the driver was annoyed when I paid our seven dollars' fare in coins which I had taken out of my piggy bank. Most of the change was in pennies. With less than a dollar left, the problem now was how to get on a flight to New York with two children.

I walked up to the American Airlines counter and ordered the ticket, which cost about two hundred dollars. Then I wrote a check. But the clerk balked.

"How do I know the check is good?" he asked. The question was ludicrous when David had put it to Eugene Ferkauf, the president of Korvette's. The question was not so ridiculous now. The check wasn't good. We had opened an account in a Bank of America branch in Los Angeles, but the balance was in pennies. The airline clerk had no way to find that out, though, because this was a weekend, and he couldn't call the bank.

"Can't you believe me?" I pleaded.

He said he was sorry. Then I had a thought. I asked the clerk to call our friend, Ed Fodor, an antique dealer in New York. "He will verify that the check is good," I said. The clerk phoned, and

Fodor not only guaranteed the check but asked to speak to me. I told him what had happened to David and that I was virtually penniless.

"Don't worry, darling," he said, "take a taxi from the airport to the Sheraton Motor Inn. I will leave money there for you."

Our plane landed in Newark in a blinding snowstorm, and it took nearly two hours to reach the Sheraton, on Manhattan's West Side. I found fifty dollars waiting for me at the registration desk. I paid the cabbie and took Cecilia and Frédéric up to the room Fodor had reserved for us.

The next morning I called a motel baby-sitter to mind my children and went to visit David in the Tombs, the city's principal jail in downtown Manhattan, where David had been incarcerated after his arraignment.

"It hasn't been so bad," David told me. "Do you know that when we landed in New York Joe Stone and his detectives took me to an Italian restaurant on Baxter Street for a big feast. And I know why he did it—he wanted to loosen my tongue. I didn't tell him a thing, but I think Stone is following the right approach. If he keeps dining and wining me, I may end up telling him everything. . . ."

I was beside myself. I wanted to know what I could do to get him out of jail.

"Raise the bail," David said blithely.

"How much is it?" I asked.

"Only fifty thousand dollars," David answered. I choked.

"Where will I get that kind of money?" I wanted to know.

"Go to our friends," he suggested.

David was mad. I didn't even have money to buy food, let alone retain an attorney to represent him. And he was asking me to raise fifty thousand for his bail.

That's the kind of guy David Stein was. He had unmitigated gall.

22

DAVID PAINTS CHAGALLS
IN THE D.A.'S OFFICE

As the days and weeks went slowly by, I tried desperately to find someone to post David's bail. I called Janine Wolkenberg. She couldn't even talk lucidly. To my everlasting shock, I learned that she was dying of cancer. I phoned Nat and Larry Kramer, our accountants, who had rented us space in their Empire State Building offices. They were sympathetic, but their compassion didn't subscribe to the principle of parting with the fifty thousand dollars needed to spring David from the Tombs.

There was no way I could raise David's bail. He remained in confinement as I hopscotched with Cecilia and Frédéric from one flea-bitten motel to another. We checked out of the Sheraton Motor Inn and into the Breslin, then the Lincoln Center Motor Inn, and finally into the Roger Williams, where I decided to stay for a while.

Not long after moving in, I left Cecilia and Frédéric asleep in the room and went downstairs for a pack of cigarettes. On the way up in the elevator, I bumped into a man and said "Excuse me." My French accent grabbed him. By the time we had reached the eighth floor, where I got off, he had told me that he had served as a pilot in the army air force, was shot down over France, rescued by the French underground, and smuggled back to England.

I saw him again a couple of days later in the lobby, where we had a chance to talk at greater length. He told me his name was Pat Patterson and that he was an engineer with the North American Container Corporation. After we had spoken a few minutes, he told me he had a bottle of wine in his room.

"If you want me to have a drink," I said, "you will have to bring the bottle to my room. I have two children there, and I cannot leave them."

A few minutes later Patterson was in my room with a bottle of burgundy. But it was Patterson and not the wine that gave my spirits a lift that night. I told him all about David and the difficulty I was having raising the bail. Patterson apparently was in no position to help me corral fifty thousand dollars, but he was eager to offer other help.

"My wife," he said, "is staying out in Shoreham on Long Island. We have a few extra bedrooms. Why don't you let me call her and see if she won't take your children in so that you can work?"

Mrs. Patterson was amenable to the idea, and that weekend, in the middle of March, her husband drove me and the children out to Shoreham. I found Mrs. Patterson a very pleasant and understanding woman. Her husband had already explained what had happened to David and why our children needed a haven. She fell in love at once with Cecilia and Frédéric, and promised to care for them with the same devotion she had given her own children, who were now grown up.

Now I was free to work. Through an employment agency I landed a receptionist's job at the Cheetah, a nightclub just north of Times Square. I was employed in the office. It was very dull work, but I hung on all through the period David was in jail.

It was David's good fortune to have been a guest at the Tombs with the notorious basketball fixer, Jack Molinas. Jack was serving time for his part in the scandal that wrecked collegiate basketball in the East. He had been a star center for Manhattan College but fell into disgrace when he was arrested, tried, and convicted for shaving points so the betting fraternity could benefit on the final scores of the games.

Molinas took a liking to David and arranged to have his own bail bondsman spring David. By that time, after a series of bail-reduction hearings in the courts, David's bond had been lowered to $6,500. But even at that, bondsmen demanded collateral, which David and I couldn't provide. That was where Molinas came in. He put up the pledge with one condition—that David would have to exonerate it within a year.

Finally, on August 4, 1967, David was released. He walked into my arms in the office of the bondsman, Al Newman. Between the time he was turned out of the Tombs and the time I met him at Newman's, David had been taken on a side trip to a hearing of the Immigration and Naturalization Service, where he had been adjudged an alien who had overstayed his welcome since entering the United States from Canada. Newman posted another $2,000 bond to spare David from commitment to the Federal House of Detention.

Our first goal upon David's release was finding an apartment. The room at the Roger Williams was too confining for four people, since we planned to bring Cecilia and Frédéric back from Shoreham to live with us. While we were house-hunting, Mr. and Mrs. Patterson invited David and me to stay on the Island with them. About a week later we found a comfortable three-bedroom house in Forest Hills, not far from our old apartment in Rego Park, except that this was a private Tudor-styled house in one of the city's most exclusive sections. The rent was three hundred a month, and we were assured of occupancy until Christmas, when the house was to change hands and be made available for the new landlord.

In the meantime, as David waited to be told when he would go to trial, he had to make a living. He found he couldn't do anything as an art dealer because his name was mud. And most certainly he couldn't dare to paint and sell forgeries, for the D.A.'s men were watching him like hawks. Yet the only thing David could do was paint. So he painted.

But with a difference. While he produced Chagalls, Van Dongens, Picassos, Marie Laurencins, and the works of the other masters he had been forging for so long, the paintings he did now were strictly on the up-and-up. A little gimmick is all it took. David was clearly labeling each painting with the legend "In the style of" whatever master he was emulating, and signing his own name to the work.

But what a different ball of wax when David trod the

straight and narrow. A Chagall or a Van Dongen or the work of any other master commanded next to nothing when it was clearly identified as an imitation. The paintings David produced under his own name were every bit as good as the ones he had been passing off as originals, but their market value just wasn't there. Nevertheless, the hundred dollars David was getting for the paintings that once went for as much as fourteen thousand was enough to sustain us.

David also picked up about two thousand dollars by writing an autobiographical article for Paris *Match*.

Meanwhile, David had had time to assess the situation and decided that the odds were stacked against him. He saw no way out of punishment, whether he made a full confession, pleaded guilty, and threw himself upon the mercy of the court, or mounted a stiff defense at his trial before a jury of his "peers." David didn't think he could find twelve men or women anywhere who could ignore the overwhelming evidence the prosecution had amassed against him.

No matter what course he took, a prison sentence was inevitable. And when it was over, there'd be no future in the United States. For as a convicted felon, Immigration would give him no consideration for a stay in this country. He would be deported.

When that day came, David knew he would be given a country of his choice to which he could be sent. But what country would have David? His native France undoubtedly would take him back, not so much for the reason that he was born there—but because he was a fugitive from justice. By then French authorities had learned about the crimes he had committed in the United States, turned up evidence of his forged sales in Paris, Cannes, and Toulouse, and the authorities were anxious to have the prodigal son returned to his native shores. David wanted to avoid that.

He decided that the State of Israel might be a very nice place to live. To pave that road for us to Tel Aviv, David sought help from no lesser a personage than movie producer Otto Preminger, who was our neighbor when we were living at 525 Park Avenue. David and I had met Preminger and inadvertently sold him a painting. It was one of our authentic pieces.

It was through Bernard Colson, back in December, 1965, that

we made Preminger's acquaintance. Colson had brought Preminger to the Trianon to show him a selection of graphics he was selling for Maeght and had been storing at our gallery. Colson introduced David and me to Preminger, but we didn't get involved in the transaction.

Then, one night Colson was to deliver a graphic to Preminger. Colson had invited me to go with him. It was bitter cold, and when we entered Preminger's brownstone town house, my teeth were chattering. Colson's teeth also were chattering, but not so much from the cold. When he unwrapped the package, he discovered that he had brought the wrong graphic. It was a work by Calder that had come out of the Trianon's stock.

Preminger was intrigued by that lithograph, entitled *Chevron noir*.

"How much is the piece?" he asked.

I said that we had it marked for $150.

"Fine," he smiled. "I'll buy it so you won't have to carry it back in the cold."

Preminger remembered him when David phoned the producer's office in the Columbia Pictures Building on Fifth Avenue shortly after the piece had been published in Paris *Match*. David had not yet decided on Israel, and his visit to Preminger was mainly to sell him the idea of expanding the story in *Paris Match* to a full-length movie. Preminger thought the idea of doing the life of David Stein on film had great possibilities, but the director didn't believe the magazine article had enough scope.

"You should write a book," Preminger suggested. "Then come back and see me." Then he added, "I'll get Jack Lemmon to play you."

Some months later, David did go back to Preminger but not with the book. David wanted to know whether Preminger could do anything about helping us to obtain visas for Israel. By then, David had been through a number of Immigration hearings, and the way matters stood, he was certain that he would be deported to France—after he had paid his debt to society in this country— unless he could get into some other country. But David didn't even have a passport.

Preminger agreed to help. He enlisted the aid of Meyer Weisgall, then head of the Weizman Institute in Re-Hovot, just outside Tel Aviv, and a good friend of the director. Weisgall agreed to do what he could.

Meanwhile, David was continuing to paint "in the style of" the masters but was getting nowhere. Sales were few and far between, and the paintings he sold barely provided us with a hand-to-mouth existence. My Christmas present to David that year was the announcement that I was pregnant again. When we finally had to leave our house in Forest Hills, we moved into smaller quarters in Sea Bright, New Jersey.

A short time later, in February, 1968, the National Broadcasting Company decided to do a half-hour feature on David. Camera crews and an interviewer descended on our house. David discussed his life as a forger and even demonstrated his technique at the drawing board by painting a Chagall. The show, produced for *New York Illustrated*, was aired on TV a short time later. The publicity helped David enormously. Art collectors began ordering David's paintings. Things were looking up. But still, he couldn't interest any gallery to hold an exhibit—and that's where the money is: mass sales.

Our summer in Sea Bright was terrible. David was to go to trial in August. Each day leading into the next was sadder. The ninety-seven-count indictment that the New York County grand jury had returned against David appeared to get ever more formidable as the moment of truth grew nearer.

Then came August. The trial was taken off the court calendar because the prosecution wasn't prepared to proceed. But I was ready to proceed—and have my baby. On the morning of August 5, 1968, I awakened David, as I had done twice before in my pregnancies, and told him I was ready. He called a cab, and I went to the Long Branch Medical Center by myself. David had to stay home and mind Cecilia and Frédéric.

My competent obstetrician decided that I had to give birth naturally because the baby was two months premature. I had to go through the contractions to help the baby's birth.

The baby was born at 10:16 that morning and weighed four pounds, two ounces. We named him Jason. And he was placed in an incubator.

David, who'd never been at the hospital when I gave birth, visited me that night with dreadful news.

"Well, *chérie*," he said sadly, "it's all over. I'm going to jail tomorrow."

"Why?" I cried in utter shock.

"Because Jack Molinas has called for his collateral, and I have no way to raise the bond."

I felt better after David's philosophical outlook on the situation.

"Even though I haven't been sentenced," he explained, "the time I spend in jail now will be credited to the prison term I receive. It is better that I do the time now than later. I have left about fifteen paintings at the house, and I will continue to paint more in jail and send them to you. Pretty soon you will have enough to get a David Stein exhibit somewhere."

Then David kissed me and said, "*Au revoir, chérie*, visit me when you and Jason leave the hospital."

I left the hospital two days later, but Jason remained in the nursery for premature babies for another week before I could bring him home.

When I paid my first visit to David in the Tombs, I found that he had figuratively taken over the jail.

"They have given me my own private cell, a bigger light bulb, and even provided me with a drawing board," David laughed. "I have already painted three Chagalls and two Braques."

David was being given special treatment, because Assistant District Attorney Stone was "working" on him. And David was happy with that arrangement, not only because he was being given special privileges that enabled him to paint and make money in the Tombs, but also because he felt by being cooperative and, as he put it, "spilling my guts out," Stone would recommend leniency.

David was giving Stone statements by the ream about his sales of forgeries. David often spent an entire day at the D.A.'s office giving sworn testimony about which gallery, which art dealer, which collector, he had sold his fakes to. It got to the point that David finally complained to Stone.

"You know, Joe," said David, "I don't mind you bringing me here, and I don't mind giving you statements. Confession is good for the soul. But you are keeping me away from my drawing board."

"If that's all that's bothering you, David, I'll arrange it so that you can paint here," Stone said.

And so on many of David's subsequent visits to the Criminal Courts Building, Chagalls, Picassos, Marie Laurencins, and other works came to life in the district attorney's office. David didn't mind answering questions and making statements now—so long as he could paint while doing that.

By January, 1969, David had told Stone all that he wanted to hear.

"Well, David," the prosecutor finally told him, "we've got a date in court for your pleading."

The plea was guilty, and three weeks later David was sentenced to three years in a state correctional facility, Sing Sing Prison, up the river in Ossining, New York. But his transfer from the Tombs was held up because Immigration had scheduled more hearings to determine where David was to be deported after he had finished his sentence.

Israel remained David's only choice until he received the bad news from Otto Preminger—that Israel had turned David down because of his criminal record. That left David no choice but to go back to France. Faced with that inevitable turn and the prospect of more years in jail there, David appealed to Stone.

"Let me go back now," he pleaded. "I want to pay my debt in France, too. If you consider all the time you've had me locked up here, I'm at least entitled to be released for time served and good behavior."

Stone counted the time David had been in confinement.

"You may be right, David," he said. "I'll see what I can do."

In June of 1969 Stone did do what he could. He got David released from the Tombs, his sentence satisfied by the eighteen months he had logged in the jail. David walked out into the bright sunshine of freedom—handcuffed to a Federal marshal, who took him to the Federal House of Detention. He was being held as an alien who had entered the country illegally, and it was only a matter of time before he would be deported to France. David didn't like it in the Federal lockup. They wouldn't let him paint.

But the works he had produced in the Tombs—some fifty-five paintings—and the ones he had done at home were enough to shape an outstanding exhibit that was held at the Wright Hepburn Webster Gallery in London. Some of England's most noble citizens attended the opening and gobbled up David's imitations of the masters, clearly labeled so, in a record-breaking sixteen minutes.

Besides the seventy paintings that were sold, I received orders for fifteen more David Steins. Among those who placed orders was Princess Alexandra of Kent, who arrived at the gallery after the paintings had been sold out. She ordered four.

The proceeds of the sale amounted to roughly four thousand pounds, or about eleven thousand dollars. With the gallery keeping 40 percent and David getting 60 percent, I received something like a thousand dollars, which helped a bit to sustain the children and me. The rest went to David for his defense in Paris.

On August 5, 1969, Jason's first birthday, I left him and the other children with a sitter, and a friend drove me to Kennedy Airport. We had first made a stop at Immigration and Naturalization's headquarters on West Broadway in Manhattan, but I was refused permission to ride out to the airport with David.

I finally saw him at the Pan American terminal. With two Immigration men guarding David, I was allowed to talk with him for fifteen minutes before it was time to board the plane for Paris. David had given me instructions to wind up all our business affairs.

"It should not take more than a couple of months," David said. "Then I want you and the children to come to France. I will not be in prison too long. We will be together again, *ma chérie. . . .*"

Then he kissed me. That was the last time I saw David.

I didn't leave the United States as David had asked. I remained on because I felt the children and I would be better off in America. One of the main reasons for my decision was the letter from David after his trial in Paris and sentence to three years in prison. He told me that he was being allowed to paint in his cell and that I could expect more paintings from him. He wanted me to arrange an exhibit of his "in the style of" works in New York.

I quickly made arrangements with the Wright Hepburn Webster Gallery in New York. Due to the fabulous results of David's London exhibit, the gallery agreed to hold a showing for us in

November. But as the deadline approached, I suddenly found that I couldn't deliver enough paintings for an exhibit. I had only about fifteen. We had to cancel the showing.

As I told you at the beginning, I do not believe that David committed a crime serious enough to warrant his imprisonment here for a year and a half and two more imprisonments in France. He did not take anyone's life, nor had he harmed the hair on anyone's body. He merely took people's money. But these were people who could well afford to be taken—and many of them, as I said before, knew that they were buying fakes. And the majority of them were happy to have them.

I can think of no better example of what I am saying than the case of Anchie Van Boythan, the divorced wife of Charles Revson, the Revlon cosmetics tycoon, whom we had known socially. A time came when David needed cash, and he went to Anchie to try to borrow twenty thousand dollars.

David hadn't been all that honest with Anchie, of course. When he asked her for the money, he offered to put up a beautiful Chagall pastel and gouache of a clown which David had painted and put into a four-hundred-dollar frame. She thought it was an original. So she took it and gave David the loan.

While preparing his case against David, Assistant District Attorney Stone went to Anchie's suite at the Sherry-Netherland Hotel and asked her to surrender the painting because it was a forgery and was needed as evidence against David. Anchie herself told me what she said.

"That painting, Mr. Stone, represents collateral for the loan I gave David. Moreover, the painting is my property. . . ."

As Stone started to leave, he turned and took one last glance at the painting, which was hanging over the couch in the living room.

"Besides, Mr. Stone," Anchie said before the prosecutor started out the door, "I like that painting."

The people who could afford David's paintings—and all of the people who bought them could afford them—also appreciated them.

Actually, I think there was only one person who didn't appreciate David's forgeries—Irving Yamet. But even Yamet had occasion to be put down after he blew the whistle on David. That happened when he ran into Chagall and his wife just before the mural was dedicated at the Metropolitan Opera.

"Mr. Yamet," I am told Madame Chagall scolded, "you should have known the paintings you bought were fakes. Not because they are bad imitations of my husband's work but because you paid so little for them. . . ."

I think Madame Chagall's succinct statement sums up everything I have been trying to say about David Stein's career as a forger. Nobody bought a pig in the poke, as the expression goes. They knew darned well, most of them, what they were getting.

But David was the one who paid for it in the end.

23

IN MY
LONELINESS . . .

With David gone, with the exhibit at the Wright Hepburn Webster Gallery canceled, I was left to struggle for myself. What money had accrued to me from the London exhibit was gone. I had three children, and I was flat broke.

Now came the biggest letdown of my life—I went on welfare. There was no other way. Cecilia, Frédéric, Jason, and I had to eat and have a place to sleep. We were crammed into a small studio apartment, and the Jersey City welfare department was keeping us alive.

I wasn't born with a silver spoon in my mouth, and hard times weren't a stranger to me. But I will not deceive you: I was devastated by my plight. There, not too long ago, I had been comfortably ensconced in a Park Avenue apartment, galavanting about town in a chauffeur-driven Rolls Royce, hobnobbing with high society and celebrities, and living like a queen.

Now I had plummeted to this—a studio apartment in Jersey City and living on charity.

That wasn't living. It was merely an existence. I didn't intend to endure it for long, and I didn't. By January of 1970, I landed a two-hundred-dollar-a-week job at the Original Masterpieces International Gallery in New York. My experience with David gave me excellent credentials to handle the duties I was assigned. I bought works of art, commissioned artists to paint for us, supervised auctions, and performed numerous other functions.

I held that job for two years. Meanwhile, I was beginning to get back on my feet in other ways. I had moved the children into a roomy, two-bedroom apartment in a very comfortable, modern apartment complex in downtown Jersey City, just around the corner from City Hall, where the crimes spawned in this seat of municipal administration in the guise of good government far surpassed any of the frauds perpetrated by David. But how many of those crooked politicians ended up in jail or were deported?

The one thing that kept my spirits high was the correspondence from David. He wrote from Prison de Fresnes, just outside Paris, at least three times a week. I was happy to hear that David, who had gone to trial the previous November and was given a three-year sentence, had been committed to that model institution. What makes this prison unique is that it has no bars—a condition laid down by the Frenchwoman who sold the land on which the prison was built.

Letters were not the only parcels I received from David. Now and then he shipped Dufys, Chagalls, Mirós, Picassos, Matisses, Braques, and other works that he painted in jail. There was, of course, that slight difference in the signature on the paintings.

As he had done for the exhibit at the Wright Hepburn Webster Gallery in London, David made certain that he clearly inscribed the words "In the style of" on each and every work he produced, along with his own name. That made it all very legal—or so we were led to believe.

By late August, I had received nearly seventy gouaches and pastels from David, and there were enough pieces now to warrant a rescheduling of the exhibit at the Webster Gallery in New York, which had been canceled the previous November.

I was thrilled with what I saw at the exhibit when it opened on September 15, 1970, with a preview and a scheduled run that was to continue through October 3. Nearly five hundred persons responded to the 5 to 8 P.M. invitational preview, and at last, I began to hope that David had found a legitimate future in the art world.

But the next day my dreams were shattered when a gentleman

from the office of New York's Attorney General Louis K. Lefkowitz walked into the gallery just as the doors were opened to
admit the huge crowd and served Peter Wright, the president,
with a restraining order. The document had been obtained in
State Supreme Court under the claim that the paintings done
in the style of Picasso, Matisse, Chagall, and the other masters
were "good enough to fool the public into thinking they were
originals."

The fact that elections were only a month away and that the
public-relations man in the attorney general's office had phoned
the city desks of *The New York Times*, the *Daily News*, and the
New York *Post* and alerted them to the action seemed to be a too
obvious coincidence.

That order promptly closed the exhibit. But Peter Wright
didn't take it lying down. He went into court the next day, stood
before Justice Arnold L. Fein, and argued, "Nobody is going to
be fooled by these pictures. Some of them are jokes with Stein
himself appearing in them."

Deputy Assistant Attorney General Richard Scanlan protested
vigorously not only that the paintings were good enough to pass
as originals but that "it would be easy to cover that signature," as
he pointed to David's name on the sample paintings that had
been brought to court as evidence.

The judge reserved decision and declared that the paintings
could not be sold until he handed down his ruling.

No sooner had the court proceedings ended than a full-scale
controversy erupted in the State Building, where Lefkowitz and
his staff had their offices. It seems that even Mr. Lefkowitz's own
deputies couldn't decide whether David Steins were good or bad
for commerce.

Deputy Assistant Attorney General Joseph Rothman, who
headed the frauds bureau, admitted that David's works were
"damned good." He then went on to give reasons:

"The art community is very distressed that the market could be
flooded with fakes by Stein [as if it hadn't been already]. If Stein
returned to New York, after serving his sentence in France, then
I would like to see him proclaimed a public nuisance and en-
joined from painting in the style of the masters."

Another prosecutor, whose name I don't recall, had this to say in tribute of David: "Stein's paintings should go to the Fogg Museum at Harvard or to the New York Institute of Fine Arts, where students could learn the difference between originals and fakes."

I wonder how many students—let alone all the world-renowned experts who had been fooled, or let themselves be fooled—could tell the difference between any of David's fakes and the real McCoy.

Now that we were out of business, Peter Wright lamented: "We managed to sell six of the sixty-eight paintings on view in our gallery in the first few minutes of the exhibition before we were served with the restraining order. The works commanded prices of up to one thousand dollars."

He went on to say that he had expected to pull down at least $32,000 in sales for the entire exhibition.

For the next twelve days, I waited in breathless anticipation of Judge Fein's ruling. And then it came down: The court had decided against Lefkowitz's attempt to stop the exhibit. But most significant was what His Honor had to say about David:

"However fraudulent or criminal his past transgressions have been, they cannot militate against Stein's right as an artist to sell his own works, acknowledged as such."

Then Justice Fein took cognizance of Lefkowitz's reasons for trying to bar the sale of David's works—that the experts themselves had found Steins were "among the finest forgeries of impressionist and post-impressionist paintings ever made" and that "the imitating artist's name could easily be removed and the copies fraudulently resold as originals."

But the judge rejected Lefkowitz's arguments with what I think was one of the most eloquent tributes paid to my "husband": "David Stein has peculiar and unusual artistic talents. It cannot be disputed that whatever Stein's motives, he is an artist, both in terms of dictionary definitions and as a matter of practical application."

Finally the judge "unrestrained" Louis Lefkowitz's order in these words: "Not one iota of proof has been submitted that anyone is now engaged or about to engage in the removal of Stein's name for the purpose of passing off his work as an original work of one of the masters."

Thus, there was no basis to enjoin the sale.

These amicable declarations for our side by Justice Fein brought jubilation to Peter Wright and me. The exhibit was immediately reopened—but with a wary eye riveted on Lefkowitz. We suspected that the attorney general wasn't going to take the court ruling as the last word—that he would seek relief in the higher echelons of the judicial system.

So we proceeded to sell David's paintings with anxiety and haste, for we didn't know when Lefkowitz would strike back. And strike back he did, twenty-eight hours later, when his deputies applied to the Appellate Division for a reversal of Justice Fein's ruling.

Well, we were out of business again—but in those twenty-eight hours no fewer than forty persons had been attracted by the sign reading: *Forgeries by Stein*. And those forty persons also bought forty of David's paintings.

Justice did not triumph until eight months later when the five-member bench of the Appellate Court upheld Justice Fein's ruling. Lefkowitz had lost again, and we had won. The victory this time was a lasting one. The attorney general did not fight us again.

But that isn't to say we didn't have other skirmishes. David's many creditors descended on the Wright Hepburn Webster Gallery *en masse* and placed liens of nearly $200,000 against the proceeds from the sale of the paintings. But David had the last laugh on his creditors, for he had sold all the paintings beforehand to an American corporation, which had consigned the works to the gallery. The creditors were left still holding the proverbial bag.

With all the publicity resulting from Lefkowitz's litigation against his works, David had finally become a celebrity in his own right. And now the right to imitate him had passed on to others. That truism became self-evident during the exhibit at the Webster gallery when an unidentified man set up an easel on the sidewalk outside and spent nearly the entire day painting.

When he was finished, he walked into the gallery and proudly displayed his work.

"This is a David Stein fake," he declared jubilantly. "Would you like to buy it?"

24

WHERE DO I
GO FROM HERE?

David was released from Prison de Fresnes in February, 1970, after serving only six months. He was not freed but sent to Cannes to face charges of selling a forged Van Dongen and a dozen fake Cocteaus. But the complainants never showed up to press their charges, and David was sent on to Toulouse to be prosecuted on the complaint that he had sold a fake Van Dongen there.

David was convicted once again and sentenced to another three years in the prison at Toulouse. But the authorities handled his case in a very democratic manner, and allowed him to serve the sentence concurrently with the time still owed to Prison de Fresnes.

During his incarceration in Toulouse, David was allowed to paint. He decided to produce works in the style of El Greco. They allowed David to do his painting in a special part of the prison—the death cell. It happened to have been unoccupied at the time.

David donated one of his first works to the raffle of the local synagogue, then he decided that the rest of his works were to go to the church next door to the prison, because the abbé, who was chaplain of the prison, had befriended David. He shopped for the paper and paints my "husband" needed to produce his works.

David was released from the prison in Toulouse on March 9, 1972. His debt to society had been paid.

INDEX